Travelling with Tech (Android Edition)

© 2023 iTandCoffee

Who is iTandCoffee?

iTandCoffee is an Australian-based small business established in 2012, offering technology support and education – for personal and small business technology.

The focus of iTandCoffee has always been on providing patient, friendly and supportive assistance – acknowledging that technology is a daunting and mystifying subject for so many people.

While iTandCoffee has always had a strong focus on Apple devices, we also provide assistance with, and training on, a wide range of other technology topics.

iTandCoffee operates in and around Camberwell, Victoria (in Australia), and also offers support and training remotely - both nationally and worldwide.

Visit www.itandcoffee.com.au to learn more about iTandCoffee.

Subscribe to the iTandCoffee newsletter at www.itandcoffee.com.au/newsletter.

iTandCoffee Products and Services

For queries about iTandCoffee products and services – including books, videos, newsletter, appointments and more - call **1300 885 420** (Australia only) or email **enquiry@itandcoffee.com.au**.

Travelling with Technology (Android Edition)

TABLE OF CONTENTS

Travelling with Technology
(Android Edition)

TABLE OF CONTENTS

Travelling with Technology
(Android Edition)

TABLE OF CONTENTS

Travelling with Technology (Android Edition)

TABLE OF CONTENTS

Travelling with Technology
(Android Edition)

TABLE OF CONTENTS

1. About this Book

This book has been developed based on research and planning that I have been doing for a trip that my husband and I will be taking later in 2023 – research and preparations that I figured would be worth sharing with others, as I know some of the topics relating to travelling with technology can be confusing and daunting.

The book looks at general travel considerations relating to technology that are independent of the type of mobile device that you take.

It also looks at specific apps, settings and features relating to an Android device, showing screen shots from a Samsung Galaxy smartphone.

It must be noted that Android device settings and options can vary dramatically across brands, models and versions of the operating system - so the screens shown are intended to provide some guidance on where to find various features and settings but may not exactly reflect your own device.

The topics discussed in this book do assume at least a basic understanding of mobile phones and tablets - things like SIM cards providing access to the mobile phone and data network, and the difference between using Wi-Fi and mobile data for internet usage by a mobile device. If you need further grounding on these concepts, refer to the iTandCoffee book **Getting Connected** (see www.itandcoffee.com.au/store/c180/technology-basics).

This **Travelling with Technology** book does not seek to provide any definitive advice on 'must-dos' and 'must-haves'.

Instead, it provides suggestions, ideas, and alternatives to consider. It is certainly not intended to be an exhaustive study of this topic.

Most importantly, all readers must understand their own service provider's offering in relation to mobile services abroad – in terms of any costs, limitations and conditions associated with these services.

For readers who are from countries other than Australia, you will notice that the references to International Roaming in this book are about Australian telecommunication companies.

Similar offerings are most like available from companies in your own country. Check their websites for details.

Anyone requiring one-on-one assistance or advice in relation to this topic (or any other technology topic) can contact iTandCoffee at enquiry@itandcoffee.com.au to make an appointment.

Or visit the iTandCoffee website at www.itandcoffee.com.au/appointment-request.html.

2. A Handy Checklist

Let's start with a summarised checklist of list of key things to consider before you travel.

Each of these items will then be explored in further detail throughout the book. The relevant chapter references are shown for each item in the list.

☐ Understand the International Roaming offering/s from your Telco for your destination/s, in terms of availability, cost, limits, etc. *(Chapters 3-5, Appendices A-C)*

☐ Know how to control International Roaming and how to choose which Roaming option should apply, via the Telco's App *(Appendices A-C)*

☐ Know how to control Data Roaming, Mobile Data and Phone/SMS connectivity using your device's Settings. *(Chapter 7-8)*

☐ Decide if you need an alternative mobile service (or services) while you travel – and purchase in advance if needed. *(Chapters 4, 6)*

☐ Consider if it is worth changing your physical SIM to an eSIM before you go (if your phone caters for eSIMs) *(Chapters 6-7)*

☐ Check out if Wi-Fi Calling is available while on your home Wi-Fi Network, so that you know how to detect if it is available when you travel *(Chapter 5)*

2. A Handy Checklist

☐ Understand the dangers of public Wi-Fi and how to stay safe – and install a VPN to ensure that safety *(Chapter 18)*

☐ Prepare your devices by turning off mobile options that could unintentionally use data (unless you are not concerned about data usage) *(Chapter 8)*

☐ Make sure your device has enough storage for all your travel data, apps, photos – delete (or offload) unwanted apps & data *(Chapter 9)*

☐ Is the device's battery OK? Does it need replacing? Do you need to take a portable charger? *(Chapter 9)*

☐ Have all available software updates been applied? *(Chapter 9)*

☐ Pre-download necessary apps, translations, maps, city guides *(Chapter 15, 16, 19))*

☐ Get the apps associated with all your flights, accommodation, bookings, tickets, etc. *(Chapters 12-14)*

☐ Get your itinerary into digital format – all stored so that internet is not required *(Chapter 15)*

☐ In advance, test out the messaging and internet calling apps you will be using with the key people with whom you will need to have contact while travelling *(Chapter 10-11)*

☐ Pack those travel accessories, adaptors, charges, cables – including a SIM pin (extractor) if needed *(Chapter 17)*

☐ Money – will you use a travel debit card? Get the app/s, know how to load currency, consider pre-loading when exchange rate is good. Get a currency conversion app. *(Chapter 20)*

☐ Think about your travel photos? Do you have enough storage on your device and in your Google account? *(Chapter 21)*

☐ Check that your Camera app will store the location of the photos that you take *(Chapter 21)*

☐ Pre-load entertainment (movies, series, podcasts, books) *(Chapter 22)*

☐ Install and activate the Google Find My Device app – and know how to find/lock/erase a lost device *(Chapter 18)*

☐ Make sure you know your Google account and password - in case you need to access Find My from someone else's device. *(Chapter 18)*

☐ Get those passwords into a form that is paperless! And make sure your device has a good Passcode. *(Chapter 14 & 18)*

3. Keeping Connected when Travelling

First, what are your phone & text needs?

When considering your mobile phone and text requirements while travelling, there are some key questions to consider:

- Do people from home need to call you? How often?
- If yes, does it matter if they must phone you on an international number?
- Or do you need an Australian number to avoid high cost to callers? Does this number need to be your usual mobile number?
- Will you need to call home? How often?
- Do you need a phone for local calls at your destination - to contact travel companions or to arrange tours, accommodation, etc.?
- Do you need to send SMS's? How often?
- Are you travelling with someone else who will have phone/text access?
- And could you just survive with internet messaging and calling?

You may not need a phone service at all!

For many trips, no Phone / SMS capability is needed – or at least is rarely needed.

You can consider managing the whole trip using messaging and internet calling apps (e.g. WhatsApp, Facebook Messenger) and (maybe) Wi-Fi Calling (something we'll cover soon).

All these methods of communication need is an internet connection – and this can using be free Wi-Fi at hotels and other accommodation, Airports, Cafes, and even sometimes while in transit on trains, in buses and other places.

3. Keeping Connected when Travelling

But best to never say never!

It is important to consider the scenario where you ***do*** need to make a phone call – perhaps a lengthy call – to back home.

What if your credit card gets blocked and you need to call your bank! Or there is the need to call someone in the country in which you are travelling.

In the case of the bank, you could be left on hold for lengthy periods - so you need a phone service that won't cost a fortune for the amount of time you need to be on calls.

And is there a chance you might need to receive a text code to authorise a new payee or to sign-in to an account? You will need your home SIM to be in your mobile device to receive such a text.

For your home mobile plan, what options do you have?

If you take your mobile phone with your home SIM, you can use something called **International Roaming**, which we'll talk about in more detail shortly.

Basically, it involves using your phone's usual SIM card when you travel for phone calls, SMSs, and mobile data – at an extra cost.

International Roaming may well be enabled by default for your mobile service, but you may need to check in advance (with your Telco) to make sure it is available and learn how to enable and disable it.

Telco websites provide such information – or you can call or visit your Telco to discuss what is available to you. The app associated with your mobile service will also usually show what Roaming service is available. We discuss three Australian Telco apps in the Appendices.

3. Keeping Connected when Travelling

These days, International Roaming is usually available in two forms:

- **Day packs/passes/add-ons** that mean you a incur fixed daily charge (unless you use too much mobile data, in which case extra charges apply)
- **Pay As You Go (PAYG)**, where you pay by the minute for phone calls (both in <u>and</u> out), outgoing SMSs, and for any mobile data you use. (Note that MMS text messages with images etc. use mobile data. An SMS can only contain text and basic emojis.)

So you will need to understand what is available for the plan you have with your Telco and for the location/s you will visit: what are the costs, conditions, restrictions, etc. and how you can control which option you will use.

We will discuss the options for each of the major Australian Telcos shortly.

Other Alternatives to using your home SIM

If you discover that the charges associated with International Roaming using your home SIM will be too expensive, there may be other cheaper options available.

You may be able to pre-purchase a SIM for your destination/s before you go.

This could be a Pre-Paid SIM with a 'roaming pack' from a Telco in your home country.

Or you can get a special 'Travel SIM' that you purchase online, as either a physical SIM card or as something called an eSIM[1] (if your phone supports eSIMs).

Another option – which is often the cheapest - as long as you are staying long enough in each country – is to purchase a local SIM or eSIM at your

---

[1] eSIM stands for embedded SIM and is a SIM card that is built in to your device – instead of a separate physical SIM that you insert. Devices with eSIM capability will allow multiple eSIMs to be added, although only one eSIM can be active at any given time.

3. Keeping Connected when Travelling

destination. You may also be able to purchase a multi-country SIM at that destination (depending on where you are travelling).

Choosing the best solution for your own travels will depend on where you are going and what SIMs are available for these places, how long you are staying in each place, how contactable you need to be, how comfortable you are about buying at your location, and a few other parameters.

We will look at these alternatives in more detail shortly, discuss some options, and look at why you might choose one over the other.

And what are your Internet needs?

In addition to your phone needs, you will need to consider your use of internet while you travel – for checking emails, looking up tours, messaging using apps, using mobile banking, entertainment, and so much more.

Will you only need/plan to use internet at your accommodation and/or use public Wi-Fi available at cafés, airports, and other places?

Or will you need internet when you are away from Wi-Fi - for example, for navigation, translations, messaging and more when you going from place to place?

If you need mobile data on the go (away from Wi-Fi)

Why might you need internet when you are away from Wi-Fi? If you want to

- use your phone for **navigation**, internet is needed to refresh the maps as you move (unless those maps have been downloaded in advance).
- use **OK Google** – perhaps for translation or information about your location – you will need internet.
- **translate** signs or converse in another language, you will need internet for these translations (unless you have downloaded translation files in advance).
- **message** travel companions (or family/friends back home) while on the move – using internet messaging apps/features like WhatsApp, Messenger, Viber, Skype, etc. – you will need internet.
- **look up information** about the sights around you – and get directions to your next sight – you will need internet.

3. Keeping Connected when Travelling

If you think you might need internet on the go, consider how often might you need it? And how much data you might need (which will depend on the sorts of things you need to do).

As mentioned for a some of the scenarios above, there is always the option to pre-download data that you might need 'on the go', so that mobile internet won't be required too often (or at all). We will look at some examples of this in later chapters.

All of these considerations will help determine which of the following options (one or more) will be best for accessing mobile internet as you travel:

- Use your usual SIM with Data Roaming.
- Pre-purchase a SIM or eSIM for your destination/s (data only or with phone and text too).
- Buy a local SIM or eSIM at your destination.

Online Safety considerations

An important consideration when thinking about how you will access the internet during your travels is **staying safe online**.

Public Wi-Fi networks are notoriously unsafe. Even your hotel's Wi-Fi may not be completely safe.

Using your phone's SIM card to access the internet will always be safer than any public Wi-Fi network – so this may drive your decision around the best option for internet access during your trip.

We cover the topic of safety in more detail in a chapter 18. where we discuss how you can keep yourself safe on public Wi-Fi – if you do decide to go with that option at any point during your travels.

But first we will look at (in general) International Roaming using the main Australian Telcos. The Appendices at the end of this book then show further information about the Telco offerings that applied at the time of writing this book.

4. Which Option/s Should I Choose?

Let's take a bit more of a look at the options you might choose for phone and internet when you travel, depending on your requirements. In subsequent chapters, we will then look at more detail the various options.

I need my home number for calls and texts

Choose International Roaming with the daily fee from your home Telco.

This is most definitely the easiest option – if you can afford it!

But it can become very expensive if you are going on a longer trip. For example, a 30-day trip roaming with Telstra would cost $300 (assuming the roaming is used every day and you choose their daily roaming fee option).

International Roaming will be too expensive

Even if you decide that International Roaming is not your preferred option because of cost, it is still a good idea to have access to international roaming during your trip – even you just use it very occasionally.

On most days, leave your phone in Flight mode – or even consider taking out (and safely storing) the SIM card to avoid any charges on that service. Just

4. Which Option/s Should I Choose?

use public and accommodation Wi-Fi. (And of course you'll need to make sure to take the little pin for popping out the SIM if applicable to your phone.)

If you have more than one SIM in the device, you can just turn off the home SIM to avoid any charges. Same applies for any other eSIM you install.

Also **leave Data Roaming turned off** most of the time in the phone's Mobile Settings, and only enable this if you definitely need to use mobile data. If you have multiple SIM installed, this Data Roaming setting will need to be managed on a per SIM basis.

We'll cover all these settings in more detail from page 36.

Consider only enabling the 'daily pass' type of international roaming on days that you want to use it for several things. Otherwise, stay in Flight Mode with data roaming and mobile data turned off – and even turn off the Day Pass option in the Telco's app (if applicable).

If you just need to send a quick text or make a quick call while 'on the go' – or perhaps even just catch up on texts (SMSs) you have missed – consider that PAYG may be cheaper than your Telco's daily charge.

Receiving texts is free. PAYG charges only apply for calls in and out, for outward SMSs, and for mobile data (including MMS's).

Also consider that there may be the option of **Wi-Fi Calling** when you are connected to Wi-Fi – which does not involve any roaming charges if calls (or texts) are made to your home country while this is active. We describe Wi-Fi Calling in more detail in the on page 27.

And if you do need to be contactable by phone while travelling but don't want to (or can't) use your home service, consider a pre-purchased travel SIM that covers your destination/s – a selection of which we cover in chapter 6.

Some such SIMs offer a local Australian phone number for the SIM (as well as an international mobile number) – so that those who call you from Australia will not have to dial an overseas number.

We have used such SIMs on our own travels in the past because we had family members who needed to be able to call us as often as they liked without incurring additional costs.

4. Which Option/s Should I Choose?

I need a local phone number at my destination

If you need a local number at your travel destination, you will probably need to buy a SIM or eSIM at your destination. This is often the cheapest option for phone and data (unless you are going to lots of countries).

You will only be able to use this option if your mobile phone is not locked to a particular home network. You will need to present your passport, and you may also need to provide a local address when purchasing the SIM.

Also be aware there may be network configuration steps in your device's settings to set up the SIM (to set up something called APN settings), so you'll need to know what to do. We'll talk about these settings in chapter 7.

You will often find shops at airports selling SIMs. Consider that there may be a language barrier, so you may need a translation app with offline translations (see page 77)!

And SIMs purchased at the airport may not offer the best value when compared to those you can purchase in town.

There may be the option of pre-purchasing a SIM for your specific destination/s before you travel. There are several online sites offering this pre-purchase option – we look at these in chapter 6.

But really consider what it is you need a local number for. Is it because you will need to make or receive lots of local calls?

Can you arrange things online? Is WhatsApp an option for locals to call you?

And for the number of times you need a phone, might your home service's International Roaming and its daily charge be a cost-effective option?

4. Which Option/s Should I Choose?

I will need mobile internet

If you don't want to use data roaming with your home SIM – or if you think the amount of data you will need is much more than what is available from the offered roaming allowance - you can get a separate SIM with a data allowance. If you don't need local number, this can be a data-only SIM.

If your phone supports it, consider getting an eSIM so that you don't have to remove your home SIM (but can instead just turn off the home SIM). You might want to also consider converting your home SIM to an eSIM, so that the SIM tray is free for any physical travel SIM that you purchase.

Data-only eSIMs can be easily purchased online <u>before</u> you leave, as well as during your travels. And there is an app that makes getting eSIMs super-easy. We look at this app on page 34.

If your device only supports a single physical SIM, always have your home SIM with you as backup to any travel SIM you purchase and use.

My trip will include lots of destinations

Consider an international SIM that covers the locations you are visiting. These can be purchased on arrival (depending on your destination), and some

4. Which Option/s Should I Choose?

multi-country Travel/Tourist SIMs can be purchased in advance. Or just use International Roaming with your home SIM if you can afford this.

I will be cruising

It is important to note that the $5 or $10 daily roaming day passes that most Australian Telcos offer **do not cover cruising**, even if you are close to shore.

PAYG or special cruising packs may apply and can be very expensive.

Check with your Telco if you are not sure and closely explore the option - and cost - of Wi-Fi that will be available onboard.

5. More about International Roaming

We mentioned International Roaming in general in earlier pages, so let's now explore this in some more detail.

In particular, we will look at International Roaming using the three main Telcos in Australia – Telstra, Optus and Vodafone. If you are a reader from a different country (or using a different Australian Telco), check with your own Telco to see what roaming products are available.

What is International Roaming?

International roaming is a service that allows you to use your mobile phone when you travel outside of your home country, using the SIM card that you normally use at home.

When you are in another country and your usual network isn't available, your phone will connect to another partner network that has an agreement with your service provider.

Extra costs are incurred – in addition to any monthly plan payment - when you use that partner network.

Controlling International Roaming

If you plan to take your home mobile service with you when you travel abroad (i.e. you plan to use your home SIM card), make sure you understand the International Roaming offering from your Telco – and how to enable or disable it.

For the major Australian Telcos, the International Roaming settings for the service can be managed from the Telco website, by signing into the account that you have set up with that Telco.

But there is an easier way to manage the International Roaming settings associated with your mobile service – and that is from the Telco's App.

Get your Telco's App to Manage International Roaming

Make sure you install your Telco's app on your device in advance of your trip, and make sure you have learned how to use it before you go.

5. More about International Roaming

We'll briefly discuss these apps in upcoming chapters and in the Appendices – the **My Telstra**, **My Optus,** and **My Vodafone** apps.

Make sure before you go that you know how to check and manage the International Roaming settings for your mobile service from within the applicable App.

The International Roaming features that are available for your mobile service will depend on the plan associated with that mobile service – so also make sure you understand what your plan offers.

If it is not offering a roaming service that you need, you may need to consider making necessary changes to your plan (or consider alternatives).

Also be alert to the fact that the International Roaming services, costs, and availability will depend on your travel destination – with some destinations not covered by the 'daily pass' type of roaming that we describe, and/or perhaps incurring higher roaming costs.

For each Telco, you will most certainly incur International Roaming charges if you:

- Make or receive a phone call.
- Send an SMS.
- Access mobile data or send/receive an MMS.

It is important to note that receiving an SMS does not incur any International Roaming costs.

As mentioned earlier, you may have the option to choose a 'daily pass/pack' type of International Roaming or to Pay As You Go (PAYG) – or to turn off International Roaming completely.

Let's look at these options further.

5. More about International Roaming

Daily Pass / Pack / Add-on

We go into these in more detail for each Telco in the appendices, but here's a summary of the Daily Pass / Pack offering for each of the major Australian Telco's.

For Telstra and Vodafone, the daily charge (if this type of roaming is available for your destination/plan) will typically be

- $10 per day for Telstra (OR only $5 if travelling in NZ) and
- $5 per day for Vodafone

where the daily charge is only incurred if any of these 3 events occur

- you make or receive a phone call.
- you <u>send</u> an SMS.
- you access mobile data or send/receive an MMS.

Important: Just be aware that for Telstra, the 'day' is a 24-hour period from 0:00-24:00 AEST, so you could easily incur 2 daily charges on the one day of use overseas. Vodafone customers should check if the same applies to its daily roaming product.

For Optus, you choose to enable a daily ($5) or 7-day ($35) 'pass' as needed. The 24 hours of the 'day' (or '7-days') starts as soon as the pass is purchased.

Once the Optus pass is enabled, you have unlimited calls for that 24 hour (or 7 days).

Each of the Telco's provide mobile data as part of the day pass/pack/add-on.

For Telstra, you will have only 1GB of data for use in the 24 hours (0:00-24:00 AEST).

Optus offers a more generous 5GB for a single day pass, and 35GB for a 7-day pass.

Vodafone allows you to use your usual monthly data allowance – which could be tens of GBs. If you go beyond this data allowance, an extra charge will apply for further data use.

For all Telco's, additional charges apply if you exceed the data allowance.

5. More about International Roaming

Again, it must be emphasized that the cost, availability, and inclusions will depend on your plan and the destinations for your travel.

There may be a limit on the number of days that you can use roaming day passes.

Always check your Telco's website for further details.

An important exclusion is that the day pass/pack will **not** be available on cruise ships – even when you are close to shore.

Pay As You Go

As indicated by the name, this type of International Roaming means you will pay for

- every minute of an incoming or outgoing phone call (typically $1-$3 per minute)
- every text you send (e.g. 50¢ - 75¢ per text)
- every MB of mobile data you use ($1-$3 per MB).

Pay As You Go (PAYG) is certainly an excellent option to consider using if you just want to send a quick SMS on a given day – or perhaps make a really quick call.

In this case, it is worth considering disabling (or not enabling) the day pass/pack option and just using the Pay As You Go roaming to send your text or make or receive a very short call (and maybe receive some texts).

However, if you ever do use the Pay As You Go type of International Roaming, make sure that you are **absolutely certain** that the Mobile Data AND Data Roaming settings are disabled in your device's Settings (see chapter 7.

Otherwise, you could incur hundreds - or even thousands - of dollars in mobile data charges.

5. More about International Roaming

What if you have a Pre-Paid service?

Different options and charges may apply if the mobile service you use is pre-paid. Check with your Telco about available International Roaming options (if any) for your pre-paid SIM.

For example, Telstra offers Pre-Paid Roaming Packs that include a certain number of minutes of calls, a certain number of SMSs and a data allowance. Such packs are valid for between 3 and 14 days. But not all destinations are covered.

Optus has similar options for single and 7-day periods, as well as offering 'Travel Credit' and a 'Data Only' option that is valid for 14 days.

Vodafone offers some Prepaid Roaming Add-on options covering periods from 1 to 7 days.

Be warned that the pre-paid offerings are not available for all destinations.

See the appendices for more information about these options.

International Roaming vs Data Roaming

As already described, **International Roaming** refers to the provision of mobile phone, text, and data services by a partner network when you are not currently connected to your usual home Telco – and the type of International Roaming service you use from your Telco is managed from the Telco's app.

It is very important to understand that there is also a **Data Roaming** setting managed from your mobile phone's Settings.

This Data Roaming setting allows you to control whether your device uses the International Roaming offered by your Telco for mobile internet.

You can choose to just use the phone/text aspect of International Roaming, and not use International Roaming for mobile data – since it is usually the use of data roaming that causes unexpected (and often large) expense.

This is achieved by turning off the **Data Roaming** setting in your device's **Settings** app.

5. More about International Roaming

Enabling and disabling the phone/SMS service (as well as mobile data) is managed using Flight Mode.

We will look at these settings/controls in more detail in chapter 7. – at how to use them to control your use of the International Roaming services available for your mobile service.

Note. The same considerations apply for any tablet that has a SIM card for mobile data.

Wi-Fi Calling - A cost-free option for calls and texts?

There is a relatively new feature of modern mobile phones that is important to understand, particularly in relation to travel.

It is something called **Wi-Fi Calling**, and only became available in the past few years.

Not all mobile phones and SIM card services offer or support it, and not all Wi-Fi networks offer it.

But if it *is* available, it is worth considering its use.

Wi-Fi calling allows standard calls and texts to use Wi-Fi (if you are currently connected to a compatible Wi-Fi network) instead of using mobile phone towers. This is also known as VOIP (voice over internet protocol).

The **Wi-Fi Calling** setting is usually found in your device's **Mobile** Settings - if it is available on our device.

To find out if your device supports this feature – and where to find it and use it – try Googling something like **Wi-Fi Calling on Samsung A20** (replacing Samsung A20 with your own device type/model).

If you are travelling and if Wi-Fi Calling is available, you will be able to call and text those back home without incurring any daily or PAYG International Roaming charge.

This may mean that on lots of days during your trip, you may be able to avoid any roaming charge and just use Wi-Fi for your calls.

Note that (for Australians) only calls to/from Australia are free using Wi-Fi Calling. Calls to/from any other country when Wi-Fi Calling is active won't be possible - even to/from your current location.

5. More about International Roaming

They must use the mobile service and will incur a charge. The applicable charge will depend on the type of International Roaming you currently have active.

The trick is working out if Wi-Fi Calling is active because you can't always guarantee it will be.

It doesn't work on certain Wi-Fi networks, and your phone may not currently have it active for some other reason.

To check, you will need to be connected to Wi-Fi and have internet access.

Importantly, **a VPN cannot be active** if you want to use Wi-Fi Calling. (We'll talk more about VPNs, and why you might normally use one, in chapter 18.)

Make sure mobile data and data roaming are turned off, then turn off Flight Mode (assuming you have had it on to prevent any charges for the day).

Note that if someone calls you at that point – before you have worked out if Wi-Fi Calling is currently available - you may incur a daily or PAYG charge if you answer the call.

If it is active, you can safely call back home, send an SMS to someone back home, or check your Voicemail. You will not incur your daily roaming charge or PAYG charges, as long as Wi-Fi calling remains active.

Important Note: Just to re-enforce the point made a bit earlier, Wi-Fi Calling is **not** supported when you are using a VPN.

6. Use an Alternative SIM (or SIMs)

If the International Roaming option/s offered by your usual Telco are too expensive or perhaps don't provide an acceptable solution for your travel destination, there are other options available for phone, text, and mobile data during your travels.

Pre-Purchasing a Travel SIM

One option is to pre-purchase a 'travel SIM' that covers one or more destination.

There are several important considerations when purchasing such a SIM:

- Do you need it to provide a phone/text service?
- Do you want to have a mobile number associated with your home country, so that people from home can call you without incurring international call charges?
- Or do you just need mobile data?
- Does your phone support eSIMs?
- Are you prepared to use the eSIM feature?
- Do you want the purchased SIM to cover multiple destinations or just a single country.
- Does the option you are looking at provide good coverage for your destination (since not all SIMs and services are made equal).

For many travellers, mobile data is really all that is needed from a travel SIM – allowing messaging and calling using apps/internet, instead of using a mobile phone service.

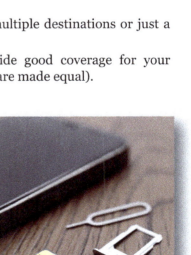

There are lots of websites offering Travel SIMs, with options for phone and text service and/or mobile data.

And if you are prepared to venture into the world of eSIMs, you can purchase inexpensive eSIMs online or via an easy-to-use App.

Let's look at some of the options.

6. Use an Alternative SIM (or SIMs)

Websites for pre-purchasing Travel SIMs

There are various websites for pre-purchasing Travel SIMs and this book will not seek to recommend any of them. Rather, this chapter is intended to offer some suggestions for you to explore yourself. I have included some screen shots taken during my look at options for a trip to Europe (as an example).

- www.onesimcard.com.au – provides a SIM (or eSIM) that can have both an international and Australian mobile number.

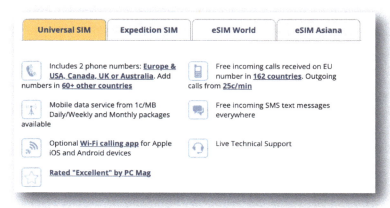

- www.simoptions.com – seems to give option of eSIM with phone/SMS service in, say, Europe – but delivery to Australia for physical SIMs looked expensive.

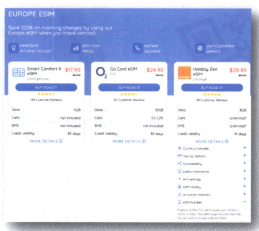

6. Use an Alternative SIM (or SIMs)

- simsdirect.com.au – both SIMs and data-only eSIMs

- simcorner.com

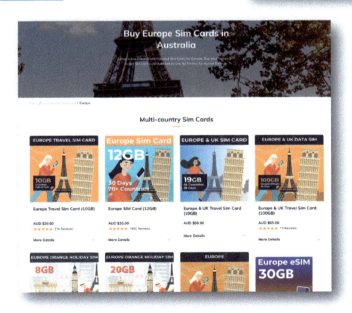

6. Use an Alternative SIM (or SIMs)

- prepaidsims.com.au

Which website should I use?

As already mentioned, this book does not seek to provide any recommendation on this. You will need to do your own research. Here's an online review that talks about Travel SIMs:

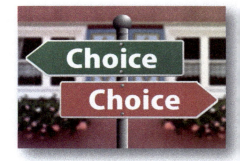

productreview.com.au/c/travel-sims

Just make sure you fully check and compare inclusions, costs, exclusions, and coverage for your travel destination before making your choice.

If you purchase an eSIM and need to install it, here is a web page that provides some instructions: *www.simoptions.com/esim-installation-guide-android*.

Another Option: Purchase SIM at destination

Purchasing a SIM at your destination will usually give the cheapest option for local calls and mobile data – and may provide larger data allowances than offered for International Roaming with your home provider and pre-purchased SIMs.

6. Use an Alternative SIM (or SIMs)

At some destinations (e.g. in Europe), you may be able to get a SIM that covers multiple countries.

For such a multi-country SIM, you need to enable data roaming to use any mobile data for the SIM – as such a SIM will generally be associated with a particular country. Using it for mobile internet in the other eligible countries requires that data roaming is enabled.

Here is a checklist of things to consider in relation to purchasing at your destination.

❑ Research where/how you will buy the SIM - at the airport (often more expensive, less options), in the town, or electronically (for eSIMs).

❑ Calls to home are international calls – this could end up expensive (unless there is an allowance in the plan you purchase).

❑ Texts to home (international) may not be included.

❑ Be prepared to do some APN configuration in device's mobile settings when you install the SIM – and know where to do this.

❑ Consider if this is really the best option if you are travelling to multiple countries, with short-ish stays in each. Will multiple SIMS be needed? Can you get a SIM at your destination that covers all the countries you will be visiting?

❑ There could be a potential language barrier when buying/setting up – so you many need a translation app (and downloaded language files to use it without internet).

❑ You will most likely have to provide Passport details and may even have to provide a local address.

❑ Don't forget you may still need your home SIM for receiving texts, checking voicemails, and making calls home.

6. Use an Alternative SIM (or SIMs)

My Preferred Option: Use an App to get a data eSIM

The option that I will be using when we next travel is to get a data-only eSIM that covers one or more of the countries in which I will travel.

I will still have my home SIM available for International Roaming, should I need it.

I have converted my usual home SIM to an eSIM, which means that I won't need to take it out and store it. I will just turn it off in my phone's settings when I don't want to use it. That SIM will have Data Roaming turned off, and this setting will only be enabled if I decide to use a 'day pass'.

I will purchase and install the data-only eSIM for my first destination just before I leave, so that it is ready to use on my arrival at that destination.

I will use an App for this purchase, one that I have tested out and found works really well.

I will then use this data-only SIM during my trip to message and call friends and family, using a combination of WhatsApp and Facebook Messenger. I will also use it for navigation and translation.

If needed, I will purchase another one of these data-only eSIMs for other locations.

This will be far cheaper than paying over $300 for a month's International Roaming with Telstra.

Using an App to purchase an eSIM

If your mobile phone supports eSIMs, there is a handy app that makes it really easy to purchase a data-only eSIM for anywhere in the world.

It is called **Airalo** and it can be downloaded from the App Store.

6. Use an Alternative SIM (or SIMs)

It allows for the purchase of **Local eSIMs**, **Regional eSIMs** and **Global eSIMs** (options along the top of the screen, below the words Hello, Lynette).

It is worth trying out this app first. To do this, you can purchase a 7-day eSIM for here in Australia for only US$4.50. This SIM will connect using the Optus network.

After purchase, the app will install the eSIM for you – allowing you to see how the eSIM looks in your Mobile settings, and to see the settings for each SIM that you will need to manage while travelling.

We cover these settings next.

7. Controlling Connectivity while Travelling

To effectively manage the use of phone, text, and data services while you travel – in particular, to avoid excess charges – it is essential to understand how to control what services are enabled and disabled.

First, Flight Mode

Make sure you are familiar with Flight Mode on ALL your devices. It is an important setting that you will need to enable whenever you are flying.

What is Flight Mode?

Flight Mode is a setting available on smartphones and other portable devices. When activated, it stops all signal transmission from your device.

This means that you won't be able to make or receive calls, send or receive text messages, or use mobile data.

While in Flight Mode, you can still choose to turn on Wi-Fi and Bluetooth.

Flight Mode can be easily managed from the Quick Panel on my Samsung phone – swiping down from the top. (I have to swipe down a second time to see the plane symbol in the example on the right.)

It can also be managed from the **Settings** app from the **Connections** option.

(On other Android devices, the option may be found in **Network & Internet** – or some similarly named setting.)

Don't forget to put your tablet and computer (if you have these) into Flight Mode as well.

Flight Mode is not just relevant to when you are flying.

7. Controlling Connectivity while Travelling

It is the key setting for ensuring that your device does not incur any International Roaming charges. While your device is in this mode, no calls can be received or made, no SMSs can be sent or received, and no mobile data can be used.

If you do decide to turn off Flight Mode at any point while abroad – perhaps just to check if any texts have been sent to you - make sure that your Data Roaming (and Mobile Data) have previously been turned off. We will look at these settings shortly.

Wi-Fi on Flights

These days, flights may offer Wi-Fi - but this service still tends to be very expensive.

Even if you do have access to Wi-Fi, you will find that download speeds and data is usually very limited – so activities like streaming of movies/entertainment is unlikely to work.

Before considering using in-flight Wi-Fi, make sure you carefully check out what is offered and the cost.

Important Mobile Internet Settings

On any mobile device, there are two key settings to consider when travelling:

- **Mobile Data** – which controls whether your device can use internet via mobile phone towers.
- **Data Roaming** – which controls whether your device is allowed to connect to mobile phone services offered by a network that is not your home service provider's network, through partnership arrangements between the two companies.

If you are abroad, if Data Roaming is turned off, the Mobile Data setting (if turned on) will not result in mobile data usage – because your device will not be able to find any mobile towers belonging to your home network, so will not be able to make a connection.

7. Controlling Connectivity while Travelling

As a rule, always leave the Data Roaming setting turned off on your device/s – and only turn it on at times when you are absolutely certain you want to use it.

Let's look at where to find the Mobile Data and Data Roaming settings on Android devices. Unfortunately, Android devices can differ in their naming and location of these settings. If your device differs to those described below, we hope that descriptions will still help you work out where to find them.

Mobile Data and Roaming Settings

For a Samsung device, settings relating to your use of mobile data should found in **Settings -> Connections -> Mobile Networks.** You will have the option to Disable **Data Roaming**. On my Samsung (below), I can choose to disable data roaming completely – or allow **National Roaming Only**. If I DO want to turn on my use of International Roaming for mobile data, I choose **All networks**.

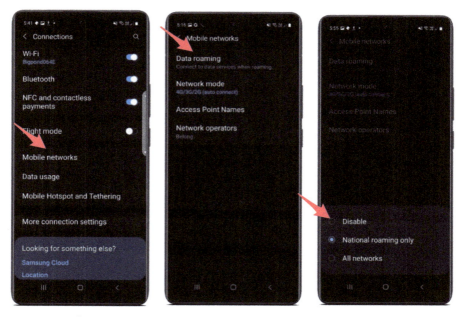

For a Google Pixel, the mobile settings are found under **Settings -> Network & Internet –> Mobile Network**.

The location of settings for managing your mobile network and data roaming will also differ depending on whether you have a single or multiple SIMs in your phone.

7. Controlling Connectivity while Travelling

If you have more than one SIM associated with your phone, you will need to manage the mobile data and data roaming settings for each SIM.

For Samsung device, this will be from **Settings -> Connections -> SIM Card Manager**.

For Google Pixel, this will be from **Settings -> Network & Internet -> SIMs.**

Once you have turned off (or on) the Data Roaming setting, then turn Mobile Data off (or on) from Settings.

A quicker way to turn Mobile Data on and off is from the **Quick panel** that appears when you swipe down from the top of the screen. (Hopefully your own phone has this feature too.)

A quick tap on the Mobile Data symbol will turn off Mobile Data, but leave Wi-Fi turned on (if it is already turned on).

If you have multiple SIMs, the Mobile Data setting is managed on a SIM by SIM basis.

On my Samsung phone, the **Mobile Data** switch is found in **Settings -> Connections -> Data Usage**

If there were multiple SIMs, it would be found in **Settings -> Connections -> SIM Card Manager ->** *selected SIM.*

On the Google Pixel, the Mobile Data switch is found in **Network & Internet –> Mobile Network**

If there were multiple SIMs, it would be found in ***Network & Internet -> SIMs ->*** *selected SIM.*

There is a quick way to get to this setting – one that hopefully applies on your own phone as well.

If I touch and hold on the Mobile Data icon in the **Quick Panel**, this takes me straight to the **Data Usage** settings – which saves multiple taps!

IMPORTANT: When travelling abroad, only return to the **Mobile Networks** settings and turn on **Mobile data** and **Data Roaming** if you are absolutely sure you mean to use it – and certainly *never turn on Data Roaming if you are using PAYG International Roaming*.

7. Controlling Connectivity while Travelling

Network Configuration Settings

If you install a different SIM (pre-purchased or purchased at a destination), you may need to adjust the **Mobile Data Network** settings in order to use this SIM for mobile internet – specifically, the APN Settings.

The steps differ for different Android devices, but here are steps applicable to some Samsung and Pixel devices. Hopefully they will help locate the equivalent settings on your own device.

1. Tap on **Connections** (Samsung) or **Network & Internet** (Pixel)
2. If you have multiple SIMs, tap **SIM Card Manager** (Samsung) or **SIMs** (Pixel) and choose the applicable SIM.
3. Select **Mobile Network** (or Networks)
4. You should see the **Access Point Names** option, which then allows the APN to be viewed and changed.

8. Controlling Data Usage

If you are going to be using mobile data, it is probably going to be very important to keep an eye on how much mobile data you use.

For example, if you are using your home Telco's international roaming day pass/pack, you will only have 1GB (Telstra) or 5GB (Optus). Or you may have purchased a roaming pack with a data allowance from a different service provider.

It helps to understand which apps are using your data – and manage which of apps are allowed to use mobile data while you travel.

Controlling which apps can use mobile data

Once again, there are differences between Android devices in the Settings options naming for mobile data usage by app.

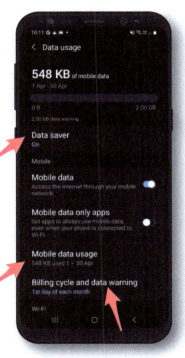

On my Samsung, I go to **Settings -> Connections -> Data Usage** to view and manage data usage by individual apps.

On a Google Pixel, go to **Settings -> Network & Internet -> App Data Usage**.

(If you have multiple SIMs, select the applicable SIM to see the usage option.)

You will see from the Samsung's screen on the right that I have the option to enable something called **Data Saver**.

Turn this to **On** when you travel.

Then, you can visit the **Mobile data usage** option to see the usage of Mobile Data by App and choose which apps can use mobile data when this Data Saver is turned on.

On my Samsung, there is an alternative way of seeing the full list of apps that can/can't use mobile data when **Data saver** is active.

Tap on **Data saver**, then tap the option **Allowed to use data while data saver is on.**

8. Controlling Data Usage

As you can see in the screen shots below, this makes it easy to scan the list of apps and turn on or off each app's ability to use Mobile Data when in Data Saver mode.

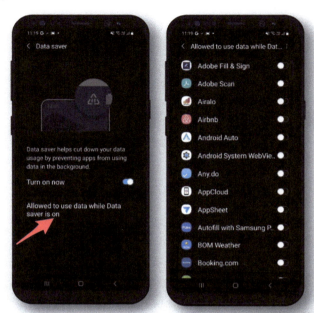

There is an option in the Data Usage area that is handy for monitoring your mobile data usage – and this option can also be extra useful when you travel.

It is the **Billing cycle and data warning** option in the **Data Usage** screen that we saw on the previous page.

This option allows for the specification of the start day of the billing cycle, and then to set up a warning about reaching a nominated data usage level for the cycle – see image on right.

You can also set a data limit for the billing cycle and cut off usage of mobile data if that limit is reached.

If, while travelling, you have a limit on your mobile data usage for a particular period, this area can be used if you want to get an idea on how much data each app is using.

8. Controlling Data Usage

If you can be bothered, re-set the **Start billing cycle on** day to the current day – which will then re-set the data usage stats.

Then, come back and reset this day when you need stats to start over.

In **Mobile data usage**, you will see the total usage figure at the top, and then the mobile data usage per app under that.

Tap on any app in the list to see the options for controlling mobile data usage.

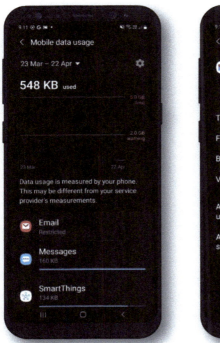 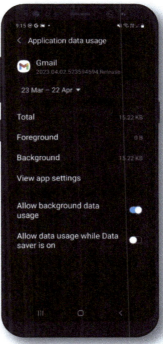

For any app that is using too much Mobile Data, turn OFF **Allow data usage while data saver is on**.

On a Google Pixel, visit **Settings -> Mobile Network** (or **Settings -> SIMs** if you have multiple SIMs) to find the settings relating to **Data Usage**.

8. Controlling Data Usage

Another way of accessing settings relating to Mobile data use by Apps is to go to **Settings ->Apps**. Tap on each app in turn to see the **Mobile Data** usage option.

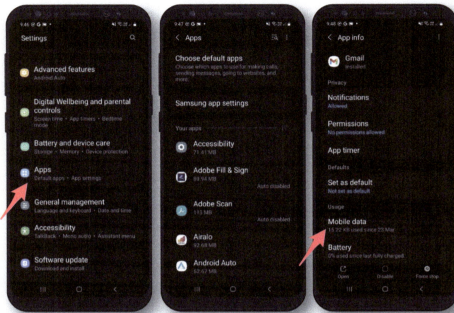

Tap **Mobile Data** to see the same screen as shown on the previous page, for managing whether the app can use mobile data while **Data Saver** is on.

My approach is to, at the start of my trip, turn off all **Mobile data** usage and **Background data usage** by my apps – and then only turn on specific apps that I want to use while on mobile data.

Monitor roaming data usage via app

Your SIM service provider's app (if there is one) will also show information about how much roaming data you have used.

8. Controlling Data Usage

As an example, on right is the information shown in the **My Telstra** app about my Day Pass, which is currently active.

This screen can be found in the **International Roaming** area of the app (found at **Services ->** *select your mobile service* **-> Extras -> International Roaming**).

You can see in the image on right that it gives a running total of my day's roaming use under the Day Pass and provides information of how many hours until the next reset (when another $10 will be charged if I use any roaming services).

If you have used an app like Airalo to purchase and install a data-only eSIM, the total roaming usage can be viewed within that app (see image below).

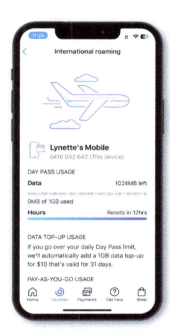

These apps are definitely very useful for monitoring the roaming data usage, and for working out when any usage period is ending.

But I also like to use the statistics in my device's settings at first, to at least gain a more granular understanding of my phone's data usage by app.

This area can also be useful in advance of your trip, to gain an understanding of how much mobile data certain apps uses – for example, Google Maps for navigation.

Test this out by using the app with Wi-Fi turned off and see how much usage it clocks up.

8. Controlling Data Usage

Some other big data users to consider

Is your device set to apply Automatic Updates to its apps?

This can be controlled this from the Google Play app.

Tap the profile circle at top right, then tap **Settings->Network Preferences** to see several options.

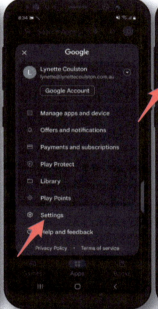

These options are **App Download**, **Auto-update apps** and **Auto-play videos**.

Tap each in turn and choose **Wi-Fi only** – or, for app auto-updates, choose **Don't auto-update apps**.

8. Controlling Data Usage

Another big user of mobile data and data over Wi-Fi can be your backups and data sync – especially your syncing of photos.

We look at the top of backups and photo syncing from page 100.

What about other devices?

If you are taking a device other than your mobile phone on your travels (one that doesn't have its own SIM), if you need that device to access the internet when you are away from Wi-Fi, you may want to give the device access to your phone's **Mobile Hotspot**.

Your phone's Mobile Hotspot allows your phone to become a portable router, providing a Wi-Fi signal to other devices.

The other devices join the hotspot from their Wi-Fi settings area, thereby giving them access to the phone's mobile internet connection.

Computers tend to use a lot of internet data for all sorts of things, so you need to be very cautious about connecting to the Hotspot of a device that is currently using mobile data and data roaming.

And your tablet could use a lot of data for various things, unless you have gone through and turned off all sorts of features (many of which are discussed earlier in this book).

Streaming of content on any device can quickly clock up big amounts of data usage.

To be safe, it is best to leave your phone's **Mobile Hotspot** setting turned off - unless you really have a critical need to be using it.

On the Samsung, the settings relating to Mobile Hotspot are found in **Settings ->Connections -> Mobile Hotspot and Tethering**.

(Note. Not all mobile services provide such a Mobile Hotspot capability. If the options in this area are greyed, and unable to be adjusted, it means that the feature is not available for the currently active SIM card.)

9. Device Preparations

Before you leave on your trip, it is important to consider some key preparations for, and considerations about, your device.

How is your Battery's health?

Make sure to check the health of your device's battery before you go.

On my Samsung, I go to **Settings -> Battery Health & Charging -> Battery**.

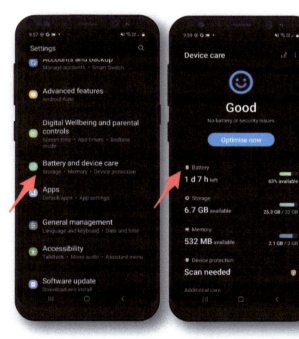

If you need to conserve battery while travelling, put your device into **Power Saving Mode –** found in your Battery settings area.

Power Saving Mode can also be accessed quickly from the **Quick Panel** – by swiping down from the top of the screen.

Hint: The list and order of icons/buttons that you see in **Quick Panel** is managed swiping down a

9. Device Preparations

second time to see the full set on icons, then by tapping ▓ at top right, then **Edit buttons**.

Another way of conserving battery is to turn off **Background Usage** on a per app basis for all but essential apps as another way of conserving your battery life. This can be done from **Settings -> Apps**

How's the device's storage?

If you are likely to take lots of photos, want to download apps, maps, translations, and more (as we will describe shortly), then you will need sufficient space on your device.

Your device's storage may be fixed and unable to be expanded, so before you go, it is important to check your storage. You may be able to purchase an SD card to extend your storage but will need to know how to use it. (We won't cover this topic in this book.)

To do check your storage, go to **Settings -> Battery and device care -> Storage**. How much space is available?

If your available storage is getting low, there are a few options for freeing up some space.

9. Device Preparations

- Get rid of any apps you don't need on the trip.
- Remove other unnecessary space hogs – use the usage data shown for each app to work out what to remove.

You will see a list of **Unused** apps at the bottom of the screen (as shown at the bottom of the leftmost image below).

  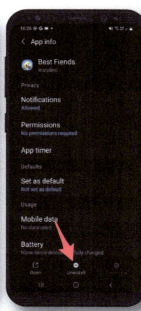

If you don't need these apps, tap each and choose the **Uninstall** option at the bottom. You may need to first turn off the **Enable** option at the bottom, to then get the **Uninstall** option.

Tap on **Apps** (see leftmost image above) to see the list of apps on your device and how much storage they use. Tap any app in the list and choose **Uninstall**, then **OK** to confirm.

If I tap the first option in the leftmost image above – **Images** – I see previews of screenshots and other images and can do a quick clean-up.

To do this, I touch and hold on one image to get a 'tick circle' at top left, and then tap to tick the photos that can be deleted. I then choose the **Delete** option at the bottom.

9. Device Preparations

Same approach applies for other types of storage listed.

Tap on each item and touch and hold on any items that can be deleted, then choose **Delete.**

If it is your Photos that are taking up significant space on your device, there is the option – if you use Google Photos – to choose to **Free up space**.

This will mean that your photos are still available to you to view. Thumbnails of the photos are shown, and you can still view any photo in the Google Photos app.

The full resolution version simply won't be stored on your device, and you will need internet to view it's higher resolution version.

It is certainly a good option if you are struggling to free up space otherwise.

9. Device Preparations

Quickly accessing frequently used information

There is a feature that I love, and that I use every day – multiple times throughout my day, in fact. And it is so handy when you are travelling.

It is a feature called **Text Shortcuts**, found (on my Samsung mobile) in **Settings -> General Management -> More typing options -> Text Shortcuts**.

This feature allows you to set up short codes that represent longer phrases, so that typing the short code results in the full phrase replacing it.

The screen on the right shows an example of one of my **Text Shortcuts.** Having set this up, when I type **eitc** and it is replaced with enquiry@itandcoffee.com.au.

For my travel, I have set **pp** as my passport number will appear. My frequent flyer number is another shortcut.

I have Text Shortcuts for phone numbers, my email addresses, my home address – and all sorts of other things.

If you get an OS mobile number, create a text shortcut so that you don't need to keep looking up the number when you need to provide it for some form or booking.

For example, set up the code OMN for that number, and only type those 3 letters to see the number magically appear.

Add a new **Text Shortcut** by choosing the + at top right of the **Text Shortcuts** screen, entering an easy-to-remember shortcut code for that phrase, and the expanded phrase. Just make sure the shortcut code is not a 'real' word, because whenever you type it, it will be replaced with the phrase.

Then choose Add.

Phone Numbers

If you do ever need to make a phone call while you are away, you will most likely need to enter an international code at the start – so you need to know how to put the + in front the country code.

9. Device Preparations

For example, to call Australia, the number starts with +61.

When you are in the Keypad option of the Phone app, touch and hold your finger on the zero to get a +. Just hold your finger on that zero until the + appears.

In most cases, you will probably just use the number stored in your Contacts list when making calls.

So make sure that the numbers of those you will call from abroad all have the relevant international code in front of them in your Contacts app (and are without the leading zero).

Get your device up to date

We will talk later (in chapter 18.) about your security when travelling – and one of the most important preparations in terms of ensuring the security of your device is to make sure that you have installed the latest version of the operating system.

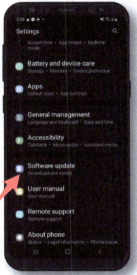

Each time there is an update, there is usually a range of security patches that plug potential security holes for our devices.

To see if there is an update available for your device, visit **Settings -> Software Update -> Download & Install**.

Get your Apps up to date

It is also worth checking that all your apps are up to date. This is done from the **Google Play** app.

Tap the profile circle at top right and choose **Manage apps and device** (see images on next page).

9. Device Preparations

The second screen below provides the **Update all** option – or I can choose **See details** to see what apps need updating and choose to update individually – or choose **Update all** to do the lot.

10. Messaging Apps

As already mentioned earlier, it is possible to get through most of your trip abroad without needing any phone and SMS service – by using Apps for messaging, audio calls and video calls.

These apps use internet via mobile data or Wi-Fi instead of the phone/SMS service.

Let's look first at the topic of Messaging using apps. We will then talk about calling.

Most Popular options

WhatsApp, **Facebook Messenger,** and **Telegram** are the three of the most popular messaging apps. Some other options are Viber, Instagram Messenger, Snapchat, and Skype.

The key thing to note when using such apps is that both ends of the conversation must be using the same App - so you may need to use different apps for messaging the different people in your life, depending on which app they choose to use.

Let's look at a couple of the most popular options.

Facebook Messenger

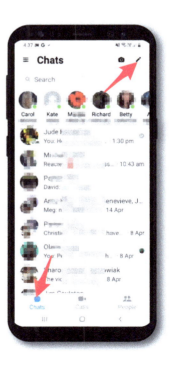

Messenger requires you to have a Facebook account to set it up. We use it extensively for family group chats – and it works very well.

If you don't want to use Facebook, you can create an account and then deactivate the Facebook aspect after setting up Messenger - and still be able to use Messenger.

10. Messaging Apps

Download the **Messenger** App from the Google Play Store.

Start a new conversation with an individual or a group from the **Chats** area of the app (icon at bottom, as indicated in previous image) and use the 'compose' symbol (a pencil) at top right to create a new chat. You will then choose who you wish to message – and this must be someone who is already a Messenger user.

Alternatively, tap on a 'conversation' already in the list of chats that appear and send a message to the person/group that way. The name or names of those associated with the conversation are shown in that preview list.

We won't go further into how to use the Messenger app here but do make sure to try it out before you go - if that is the app (or just one of the apps) that you will use.

WhatsApp

WhatsApp is one of the most popular messaging app – and is another Meta (Facebook's owner) app.

With WhatsApp, you register an account using your mobile number.

People can then message you via WhatsApp using your mobile number.

Many businesses will support communications via WhatsApp instead of phone.

Again, make sure you set up the App (download it from the Play Store) before you go abroad.

As for Messenger, a list of previous conversations is shown when you tap the Chats option at the top. Tap any item in the list to continue the conversation with the person or group.

Or use the Compose symbol at the bottom right (indicated in image on right) to send a message to someone (or a group) that you don't see in the list.

10. Messaging Apps

Make sure to give WhatsApp access to your Contacts. Otherwise, you will need to manually set up your WhatsApp Contacts.

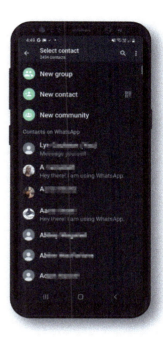

Those people who are users of WhatsApp will show a message underneath their name. If there is no such message, that person is not a WhatsApp user – so you can't message or call them using WhatsApp.

One thing to consider in relation to WhatsApp when travelling – what happens if you take out your usual SIM, so your normal phone number is no longer available? Will WhatsApp still work?

WhatsApp will continue to work even if you take out or turn off your home SIM, because it is an internet messaging app that does not use your phone service. The only problem you might incur is if you need to re-verify your account, which requires that you can receive an SMS.

This is another good reason to make sure you travel with your home SIM, even if you don't plan to use it.

Here's what is stated on the WhatsApp website in relation to use of an alternative SIM (or removal of the usual SIM).

> When you are traveling out of the country, you can still use WhatsApp account via mobile data or Wi-Fi.
>
> If you use a local SIM card while you are traveling, you can still use WhatsApp with your home number. However in this case, if you need to re-verify your account, you won't be able to do this while using the local SIM card. To re-verify / verify a phone number with WhatsApp, you must have the corresponding SIM card in your phone, with phone or SMS service enabled.

Make sure to test before you go

Whatever app/s you are going to use while travelling, make sure they work before you go.

Set up 'group chats' for the people with whom you wish to communicate as a group.

Start a conversation within the app/s with important contacts and groups, so that you can be sure both ends of the 'tunnel' are open and working.

11. Calling Options via Apps

Audio only or Audio and Video Calls

As for messaging, you don't need to have a phone service to be able to make and receive calls. The messaging apps mentioned above all have audio and video chat capabilities – allowing you to talk one-on-one or have group audio or video calls over the internet.

Audio calls use much less internet than video calls – but try to avoid either of these when using mobile data and roaming.

As with messaging, you need both parties in the call to be able to use the same service. Tap the **Calls** option (see images below), then the 'New Call' symbol at top right. Then search for the applicable contact and choose the 📞 symbol to make an audio call or 📹 for a video call.

Below are examples of WhatsApp (left) and Messenger (right) call options and screens.

12. Let's Talk Flights

In the next couple of chapters, we will talk about flights and accommodation. We will not try to give an extensive coverage of either of these topics, but rather will offer some suggestions for websites and apps that are worthy of consideration.

Google Flights

Google Flights is a handy tool that allows you to explore flights, see prices across various providers, use filters to help with selection of your flights, and then track prices over a period of time.

You can look up one-way, return, or multi-city flights.

In fact, the site www.google.com/travel offers lots of other travel-related curation topics – hotels, holiday rentals, train tickets, things to do, and more.

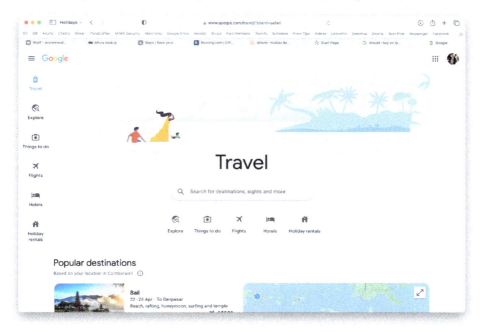

For the flights option, when you pop in your destination and click on the departure date field, you will see calendar of dates and prices – allowing you to see which departure and return dates offers the cheapest flights. (See next page for examples.)

12. Let's Talk Flights

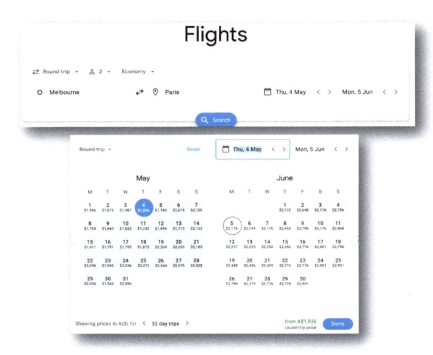

When you Search, you will be presented with a list of 'departing flight' options – and can then choose the sort order for these options, looking for the cheapest first, or perhaps the flights with the shortest flying time.

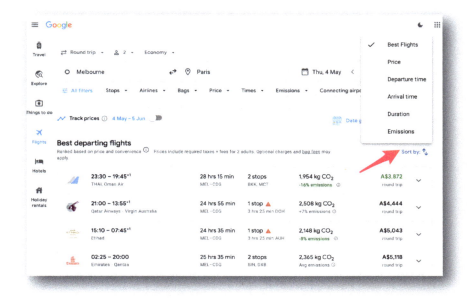

12. Let's Talk Flights

When you choose one of the flights from the list shown, you will then be asked to choose your return flight (assuming you have chosen that option). If it is a multi-leg flight, you will then choose the next leg from the options provided.

Once you have made your selections, you will be presented with the some booking options with different providers. I tend to leave Google here and look for the same flight/s on alternative sites. But it is handy for getting started.

I also use Google Flights to track flight prices over time, especially when I am booking well in advance and want to get a sense of when to book. For that, I turn on the **Track prices** switch for the chosen flight/s (indicated with the arrow below).

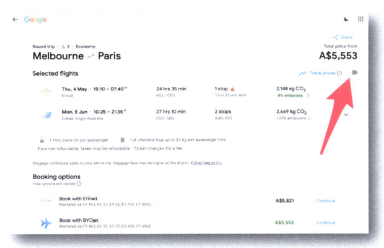

I can then monitor my tracked flights at
www.google.com/travel/flights/saves.

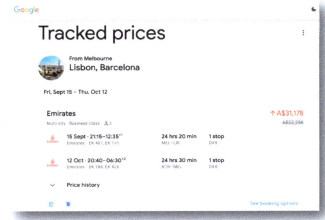

12. Let's Talk Flights

The **Price History** option shows a graph like that below. Hover your mouse over the graph to see the actual price that applied on past dates.

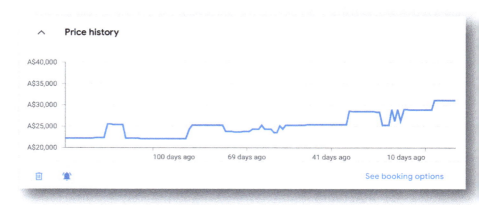

Other options

Of course, there are lots of other options for finding and booking flights online – and for tracking prices.

Some sites are 'online travel agents' – allowing you to make and manage your bookings via these sites.

These are sites such as Booking.com, Webjet, Flight Centre, and Expedia.

Others are 'aggregator' sites, curating options from other sites and presenting you with a list of option.

Examples of aggregator sites are Skyscanner, Travelocity, TripAdvisor., Cheapflights, KAYAK, Momondo.

While you may have heard reports that you should always browse these sites in 'incognito/private' mode (so that the history of what you search is not tracked and used to elevate prices when you come back to a flight), this is apparently not necessary.

Prices shown are based on demand and various other things – not your browsing history.

It is well worth comparing prices across these different sites – to check that you have the best deal, taking care to consider if you are comparing like for like.

12. Let's Talk Flights

Comparing flight options

Site Qualities	Booking.com	KAYAK	Webjet
Best	Best Overall	Best for Flexibility	Australian Owned
Price	Best	Average	Average
Flexibility	+/- 3 days	+/- 3 days	+/- 3 days
Comparison Tools	Average	Best	Average
Usability	Best	Average	Average

Here are two articles comparing online travel agent websites:

- www.flyparks.com.au/blog/best-flight-search-sites
- www.thriftynomads.com/booking-cheapest-flight-possible-anywhere

It is always important to compare 'apples with apples', and make sure you are aware of inclusions/exclusions/fees/etc.

- Beware of any servicing fee from the website (on top of the price shown).
- Is baggage included? What is the baggage allowance? Are there extra fees?
- Consider the option of booking direct with the Airline once you work out the best fare.
- Or visit a travel agent armed with the information you have researched.

Before your fly

Make sure you check with your airline if there are any restrictions on devices and other things in your carry-on and checked-in luggage.

In particular, think about any portable batteries you are carrying – are they allowed in the cabin?

During flight

Many flights these days will offer USB charging ports. So make sure to have your charging cable and any adaptor you need for the flight.

On planes or in any other public place, beware of charging ports that give a prompt on your device asking you to 'trust' them.

12.   Let's Talk Flights

Never say yes to this question if it appears on your screen, for any USB charging port you use - as it is asking for access to data on your device.

There have been recent reports that, in some public places, USB charging ports can be quite dangerous, with the potential that there may be hackers using them to infect attached devices with malware and other software.

While perhaps not such an issue on planes (and hopefully very rare elsewhere) just be aware of this concern whenever you are away from home.

I prefer to charge only portable chargers using such USB charging ports – and then use the portable charger to charge my device.

If there is the offer of a power point, this should be used in preference to a USB port – but you will, of course, need to make sure to have the relevant international adaptor for such a power point.

If you don't have any charging facility on your flight, make sure you are aware of how to conserve your battery during long flights. Perhaps consider keeping your device in Low Power Mode of turned off.

Your Tickets and Boarding Passes

Make sure you get the App (or Apps) associated with any airline you will be travelling with.

But don't just rely on website or app access for your travel documentation.

Make sure you have versions that are stored on your device, and don't need internet to access them.

A recent Ticketek meltdown at a Melbourne concert proved what can happen if you need internet or app access, and if that service is not available at the time you need access to your ticket.

12. Let's Talk Flights

In that example, those without proof of tickets had to queue up for manual tickets, instead of being easily admitted using their e-ticket.

I always save any tickets and boarding passes as PDFs. For past trips, these PDFs have been saved to Evernote or OneNote. (We'll talk about all your travel documents in chapter 14.)

13. Let's Talk Accommodation

Book Hotel Accommodation Online

As with flights, there is a large range of websites available for exploring and booking your hotel accommodation. Many travellers use this option to organise their trip – rather than engaging a travel agent.

The price of the accommodation will be pretty much the same across the board but do always check the cancellation/changes policy for the room/accommodation that you are considering.

As for flights, some websites are 'online travel agencies' – for example, Booking.com, Expedia.com, Wotif.com, Hotels.com, Agoda.com

There are also other sites that are 'aggregator' sites for accommodation - that show a range of options and provide links to jump to the selected site to book.

Some examples of aggregator sites are Google Travel, Trivago.com, Tripadvisor.com, and Kayak.com.

Here's a Choice article that is worth a read, in relation to booking hotels online:
www.choice.com.au/travel/accommodation/hotels/buying-guides/hotel-booking

Book Other Accommodation

When you are looking at Accommodation, there are lots of options other than hotels. You can book rooms, apartments, and entire homes.

Here's an article that provides a review of options for short-term rentals:
www.smartertravel.com/best-vacation-rental-sites-short-term-rental/

13. Let's Talk Accommodation

Which ones did I use?

We have just booked all our accommodation for a trip later this year, all done online using a variety of sites.

We used Booking.com, Airbnb, Expedia, and VRBO (which used to be HomeAway), and our bookings are for a combination of hotels and apartments. In a couple of locations we have booked accommodation with friends, so needed a place that would accommodate 6 people. These were booked using VRBO.

Just be careful when reviewing the options presented, as you will find that the cheapest option usually doesn't allow cancellations. If you pay a bit more, you will usually have the option to cancel up until closer to the date.

I did find that, for several searches, the options presented by Expedia didn't seem to offer cancellations.

If I liked the look of the place that I found on Expedia, I then looked it up on Booking.com – and found an option that did allow cancellation/changes.

For many bookings, you may be able to pay later – but will usually need to provide credit card details at the time of booking.

13. Let's Talk Accommodation

Take advantage of provided maps

I did like Expedia better for the maps it provided of accommodation locations, as it showed the indicative price for each place on the map.

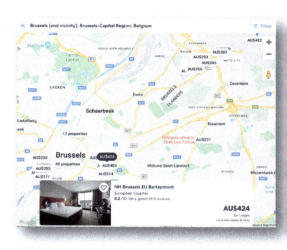

On right is such a map from Expedia. Clicking on any of the options shown provided more information at the bottom.

With the Booking.com map shown below, you must hover the mouse over (or tap) to see more details of each place marker – including the price.

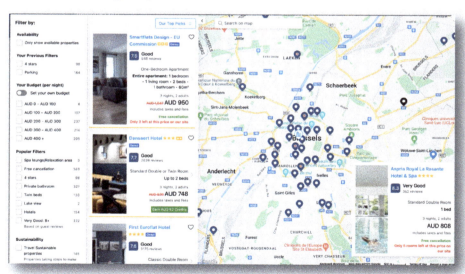

Using these maps, we would look at what we wanted to stay near (e.g. stations, city square, some attraction), then see what options were available near that/those places. The prices on the map helped us focus on the options that were within our budget.

13. Let's Talk Accommodation

Confirmations/Communications

When you book through any of these online sites, confirmation information is provided via email – so make sure to file your emails for later reference (and check your Junk Mail if you don't see such a confirmation).

Of course, this means it is important to get your email address right whenever you book something online. You will normally need to create an account using your email address.

We'll talk shortly about options for digitally storing the information about your accommodation and other aspects of your itinerary – including a particular app that does a fantastic job of collating and presenting your itinerary.

Make sure also to get the app associated with each booking site you have used – as these apps will show all your bookings and all the information you require about those bookings.

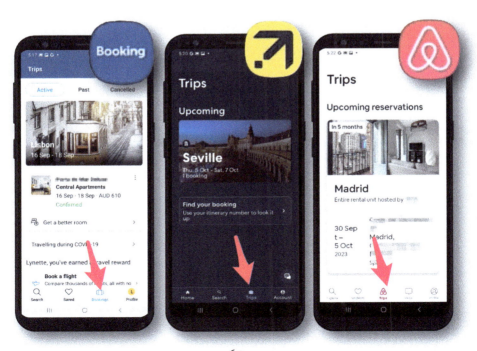

14. Your travel documentation

If you are booking a lot of your trip on your own – or even if you use a travel agent – there will inevitably be heap of documentation related to your trip.

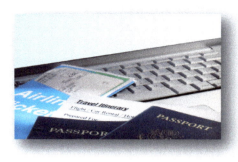

So let's look at some options for ensuring that this documentation is available to you when you need it – without needing to take wads of paperwork!

There is a huge range of options for storing your documentation – and we won't attempt in this book to provide any detail on each of the options we suggest.

Rather, if you are already a user of the suggested apps and cloud services – or perhaps interested in exploring any further on your own - it is well worth considering using one of these for storing your trip documentation.

Get documentation into digital format

Digital notebook apps like OneNote and Evernote are excellent places to store all sorts of documentation about your trip.

Evernote was my app of choice for recent trips – here is one of the Notes.

The reason why notebook apps like this are so good for trip documentation is that each Note that you create in these apps can contain anything – text, pictures, website links, files, scans, and more.

In the example right the Note contains a screen shot with lots of different typed and

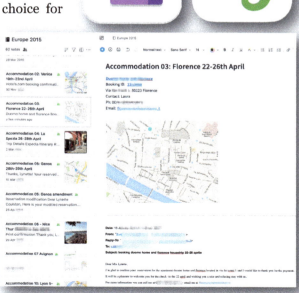

14. Your travel documentation

pasted details, plus other files and links relating to that accommodation.

As you can see, the notes in such an app can be so much more visual than just files saved as a list. They are like a digital scrapbook.

These apps allow you to use your phone to scan physical documents into the note – as a single or multi-page PDF or as images.

Scanning is also provided as an option in cloud file storage services like **OneDrive**, **Google Drive** and **Dropbox** – if you are a user of such a cloud service.

An example of OneDrive's Scan option is shown on the right.

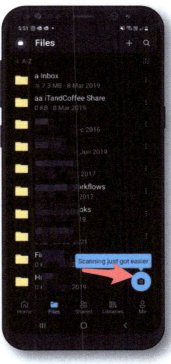

In Google Drive and Dropbox, you will find similar 'scan' buttons at the bottom of the screen.

OneDrive has a **Personal Vault** folder for securely storing sensitive documents. Consider scanning your passport and any other sensitive documents and storing them there.

Services like Evernote, OneDrive, Google Drive and Dropbox provide a free allocation of cloud storage, which should (hopefully) be enough for your trip's documents.

And if you do choose to store your files in a cloud storage service – whether that be OneDrive, Dropbox, or Google Drive, make these files are available 'offline' - i.e. that they are stored on your device and don't need internet to access them.

If they are 'on demand' only, you will not be able to open the files at time when you are not connected to the internet.

For example, in OneDrive, I must tap the ... symbol and choose **Make Available Offline** to ensure that the file is stored locally.

If you are not a user of the above apps/services, there are other great options for scanning your hard-copy documentation.

Another excellent free app for scanning is **Adobe Scan**. Microsoft also offers its **Lens** app for free.

14. Your travel documentation

We'll leave the topic of cloud storage and scanning there – as these are broader topics that are not within the scope of this book.

Contact iTandCoffee if you need to learn more about these topics, as we have videos and books covering topics like these.

Google's Keep for your general travel notes

Google's **Keep** app is another option for storing all sorts of information about your Trip.

While Keep notes can't hold PDF files, they can include text, check lists, images, links, drawings, and audio recordings.

Unfortunately, the Keep app does not support folders and sub-folders at this point, so is not the greatest app for managing a long list of Notes.

Don't forget to take those passwords

Make sure you travel with your passwords!

The best approach for managing passwords is to use a Password Safe – and there are several well-known, excellent apps that provide such a capability. Examples are **1Password**, **LastPass** and **Dashlane**.

I know many readers will have notebooks of passwords, or a page of passwords.

It is not a great idea to rely on solutions like this for your travels (or at any time).

From a security perspective is a risky approach to travel with such a notebook/paper list.

If you are a OneDrive user, consider scanning your paper-based password list into PDF format and saving it to your Personal Vault.

If you are a Samsung phone user, there is the option to store sensitive files in the Secure Folder, which is protected with a special passcode.

14. Your travel documentation

Another good option for sensitive files is to make sure you have the **Google Files** app on your device. Download it from the Play Store if you don't.

This app is great for seeing and managing all the files on your phone. It also allows for the use of a passcode-protected **Safe folder** for storing sensitive files.

Find any such files and choose to move them to this location.

Here is an article that provides further instructions for this app:

https://support.google.com/files/answer/9848742?hl=en

If none of these options are available, I would be very cautious about storing any such file containing list of passwords in an unprotected place on your phone.

A Fantastic App for your Itinerary - Tripit

An excellent option for collecting all sorts of information about your itinerary is the **Tripit** app.

Any email you receive about flights, accommodation, transport, day trips, car rentals and more can be forwarded to **Tripit** - and your itinerary is magically updated to reflect information that has been extracted from that email and any attachment it had.

Your email must be sent from the email account that you registered when setting up the Tripit app and you forward the email to **plans@tripit.com.**

14. Your travel documentation

At the Tripit end, the received email is matched to a Tripit account based on that 'from' email address, and the information in the email is extracted and added to the trip itinerary for that account.

The screen shot on the right shows an example of the Tripit itinerary for a trip we have planned.

If I tap on any of the items in the itinerary, further information is available.

For flights, it provides departure and arrival times, confirmation code, terminal numbers, seat numbers, whether check-in is available yet and more.

I can view the itinerary from the Tripit.com website – as well as from the App.

A detailed or summarised itinerary can be printed or generated as a PDF.

Of course, activities, bookings etc. can be manually added as well.

You can securely add **Travel Documents** (e.g. you passport) to Tripit, get personalised alerts relating to **Safety**, track your **Travel Stats** and more.

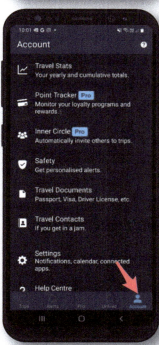

Tap the **Account** option at bottom for these options (see screen on right).

I will produce summarised and detailed output of our Tripit itinerary before we go and save this PDF securely on my phone.

This is so that I have all the information in a format that doesn't have to rely on Tripit (just in case there is any issue accessing the app while travelling).

You may have guessed that I like to have backup plans for all the documentation!

14. Your travel documentation

Tripit provides the ability to add your itinerary to your Calendar, as a 'subscribed' calendar – and makes it very easy to do this.

Simply tap Account (option on the bottom right of the app) and **Settings** option and turn on the switch at the top.

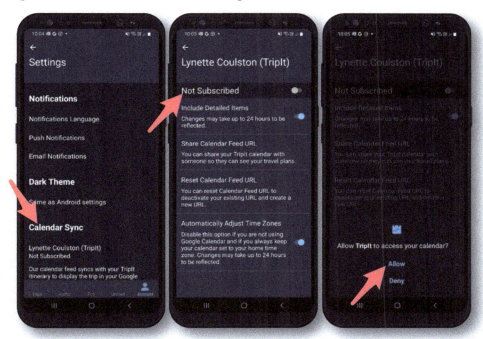

You will then need to tap the Allow option when prompted (see screen above right)

The top switch will then show **Subscribed.**

Then take a look at your Calendar app – to see all the events that Tripit has added for each of the items in your itinerary.

Note. The account to which this is added in your Calendar app will depend on your device setup. Unfortunately, that can be another whole 'can of worms' – so we won't get into it in this book.

Tripit also provides other features if you pay for the Pro version, which is $77.99 per year.

☐ Get real-time alerts on flight departures / delays

☐ Get up to date terminal and gate info

☐ A currency converter

14. Your travel documentation

- ☐ Info on Tipping customs
- ☐ Embassy information
- ☐ Language and time zone information
- ☐ Socket and plug requirements
- ☐ Required vaccinations
- ☐ Communication information
- ☐ Driving advice

Of course, there are other apps that do similar things to Tripit. Here is an article that talks about some of these:
https://www.travelinglifestyle.net/best-travel-planning-apps

Your Travel To-Dos and Reminders

Consider setting up and maintaining a **Keep** note 'tick list' of items you need to pack or things you need to do.

But what about things that you really need to remember on a particular day (and time)?

The **Reminders** app on a Samsung allows the setup of 'to dos' that have alerts associated with them, so that you get a notification about the Reminder item on a particular day and at a nominated time.

A similar app for such reminders / tasks is Google's **Tasks** app – well worth downloading and using if you use the Google suite of apps. Your tasks will then sync to your Google cloud and allow you to view them from other devices.

As an example, if you can't book certain train tickets until, say, about 3 months prior to the trip, set Reminders / Tasks for a relevant dates.

15. Speaking the language

Discovering Translation Apps

If you are going to a country where English is not the primary language, it is important to consider how you will communicate – and Translation apps offer a great solution.

Google's Translate App

Google has a translation app called **Google Translate**.

If you don't see it in your list of available apps, it can be downloaded for no cost from Play Store.

The **Translate** app allows for pre-downloading of languages for as many countries as needed – so that can then do translations at a time when you don't have internet.

To pre-download one or more translation files, tap on your profile circle at top right and choose **Downloaded languages**. Choose from the list of languages, tapping the downward arrow to download.

15.   Speaking the language

Your downloaded languages will then show at the top of the list.

Those you don't need can be 'binned' from there.

Make sure English shows as downloaded as well. Your offline translations won't work without this.

You will need to be sure you have enough storage space for any languages that you want to store, as they can take up several MB of data.

Note that if you don't want the Translate app to use mobile data, you can manage this from **Settings -> Apps** – by turning off the **Allow data usage while Data saver is on** switch in the Mobile Data option for that app.

In the **Translate a**pp, select the 'from' and 'to' languages towards the bottom.

When you find the required language in the list, tap on the name to select it.

Or choose the download arrow to download that language for offline translation (an alternative way of downloading language files – rather than going to Account area, described above).

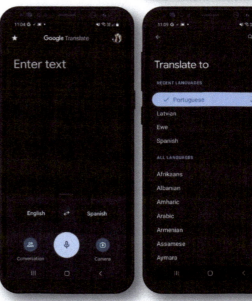

Note that, if you are not connected to the internet – or if are on mobile internet and have disabled mobile data for the Translate app – you will not be able to choose a language for which there is no pre-downloaded file.

15. Speaking the language

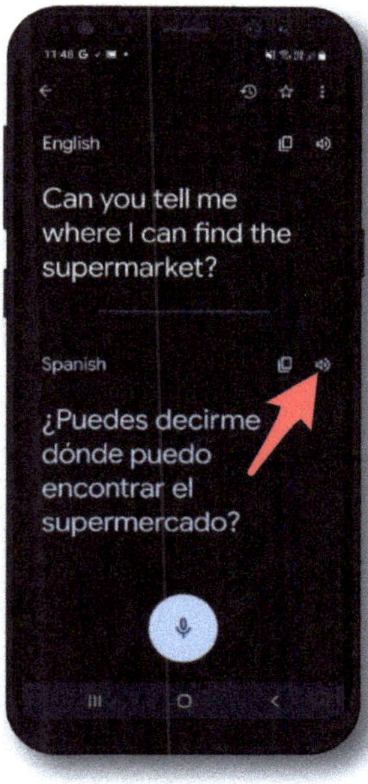

Tap the microphone at the bottom to speak your phrase or question - or tap where you see **Enter Text** to type your works (see image on previous page)

The translation will appear in the bottom section (as shown above right).

Note that the speak option offered by the microphone button will only be available at times when the app has an internet connection.

When you are using the app in 'offline' mode, you will have to type the text.

Tap the little speaker above the translation (indicated by the arrow in the image on right) to hear the translation.

If you have some further words to translate, tap the microphone again.

Or, if you typed your words, you will see the + **New Translation** button instead of the microphone. Tap this do try another translation.

The **Conversation** option at the bottom is useful when conversing with a person who does not speak your language.

Tap the **Auto** option at bottom middle to allow for each party in the conversation to speak some words and hear the translation in the other person's language.

The language of the speaker is auto-detected.

Note the **Conversation** feature only works when the app has an internet connection.

So, when don't have such a connection, you will have to type your questions and phrases from the main translation option, instead of using the Conversation option.

Set up **Favourite** phrases – one's that you might use frequently and want to avoid saying/typing over and over.

15. Speaking the language

Simply tap the star symbol at the top of a translation to add a phrase to your set of **Saved** translations (see image bottom left).

Your **Saved** translations are then found by tapping the star at top left of the main screen (see middle image below). You will see the English phrase and the translation for each Favourite. Tap to enlarge and play any of the phrases.

  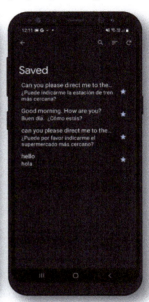

If you see a sign that needs translating, the Translation app can help.

Tap the **Camera** button at the bottom right. This will actually utilise the Google Lens app.

I prefer using the Google Lens app itself for such translations.

Download it from the Google Play store if you have not already installed it.

Select the **Translate** option at the bottom, and then point the camera at the sign (or at anything that is written in another language). Examples of Google Lens screens are shown on the next page.

You will see the translation magically appear. Tap the circle button to capture that translation.

15. Speaking the language

If the text you are viewing is in English and you want it tranlsated to another language, choose the 'to' language at the top of the screen.

If you have already taken the photo of the text that needs tranlating, tap the image thumbnail on the left of the round button to select your image.

Hand-written text can even by scanned and translated.

There's lots more to explore in the Translate and Lens Apps – but I'll leave you explore further on your own. Hopefully the above descriptions give you an adequate starting point.

Just ask Google to translate

If you currently have internet and need to do a quick translation into another language, consider using the Google bar that hopefully appears on your Home Screen.

15. Speaking the language

Tap the microphone on this bar and say something like "Translate *good morning how are you* into Spanish".

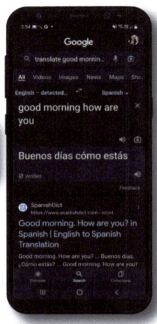

The translation will appear on the screen as text, and the Google assistant will also speak the translation for you.

Microsoft's Translator app

Microsoft also has its free Translate app.

Unfortunately, at the time of writing this book, this app does not cater for offline translations – so we won't cover it in any further detail.

Another translation tip

When you travel through Europe – especially in Italy – you will find that you come across lots of Roman Numerals. And I will be honest in saying that I am not all that good at quickly translating a number in Roman Numerals to its decimal equivalent.

For example, what year is represented by the numerals on the right?

Luckily, there is an app for that – in fact there are several.

I have downloaded a free App called **Roman Numerals Converter**.

I can type in the letters that I am seeing to work out the decimal number – or go the other way, typing in a number to see its Roman equivalent. Very handy!

16. Getting around

Using your mobile for navigation

Whether you are walking around the city, catching public transport, or driving a car, one of the must-haves from a technology perspective is an app for navigation and maps.

An essential app for navigation using a mobile phone is **Google Maps**.

Google Maps usually requires mobile data to refresh the maps as you move.

While the phone's built-in GPS does not need internet to track your location, internet is required for the map to download and refresh based on your changing location.

But what if you don't have mobile data to provide this internet service as you travel?

Pre-load Maps for Offline Navigation

As with translation files, you can choose to download 'offline' maps when you have access to Wi-Fi, so that no mobile internet is needed for navigation and maps.

Apple's **Maps** app doesn't offer this, but **Google Maps** does.

Tap your account circle at top right, then choose **Offline maps**.

You will then be able to select the Map area that you wish to download.

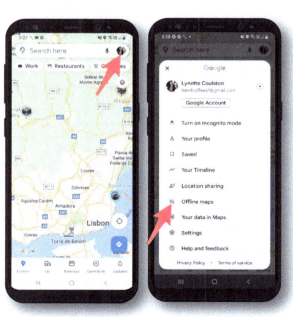

16. Getting around

Be aware that the bigger the map area you select, the larger the downloaded file – so you will need sufficient available storage for any such file.

In the example on the below (middle image), my selected map area would require 415 MB of space (and will take quite a while to download).

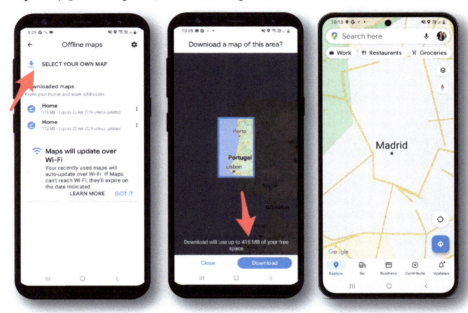

Once that Map is downloaded, I can see the area it covers by turning off my Wi-Fi and Mobile Data.

The area that is covered by the map will show more detail, whereas the area outside the downloaded region will show very little detail.

An example of this is shown in the rightmost image above, where Madrid shows very little detail when there is no internet.

Note that Google Maps won't provide transit information with downloaded maps.

Also, offline maps that you download are removed after 1 year – so you won't need to remember to clean them up.

The Offline Maps option shown above provides both the size and expiry date for each map. Tap the vertical dots on right of each map to choose to **Delete** it before this expiry, to free up the space used by the map.

16. Getting around

Other Apps for Maps / Navigation

There are other apps to consider for offline navigation, a few of which are **Maps.me**, **HERE WeGo Maps**, and **Sygic**.

I used **Sygic** on our last European trip (for driving/navigation in France and England) and it was excellent. It offers a 3-month Premium+ subscription for $19.99, so is excellent value.

Maps.ME is also an excellent free app that I will try out on the next trip.

Again, you download maps for your travel locations so that you can use the maps offline when you don't have internet. Tap on the country name to see the Download option.

HERE WeGo Maps is another app that gets a good review and that I will try out.

It wasn't so obvious how to download the offline maps in that app. You must swipe up the **Where to** area at the bottom of the screen to see more options and see the **Download** option.

Make sure for these apps that you leave the App open while the download of offline maps is completing.

These downloads can take a while. When I downloaded Spain in Maps.me, it took about 45 minutes.

City Guides

Check for any available digital city guides for the places you are visiting – and especially look for offline guides that allow you to explore and learn about the sights without internet.

Here's what came up in App Store for the search phrase City Guides Lisbon.

Also look for any public transport maps for the city. The **CityMapper** app is popular, but only covers select places – so make sure it is relevant to your trip.

16. Getting around

Consider also if you can pre-download any **Audio Guides** of key places/attractions – to save having to purchase such a guide at the location.

Getting from A To B

If you are looking at options for getting from one place to another, there is an excellent website and app that can help.

The app is called **Rome2Rio**, and the website is www.rome2rio.com.

It partners with the likes of Booking.com and Skyscanner for tickets, hotels, and car hire, and with Omio (mentioned below) for train tickets.

Below is an example of the results that I got (on the website) when searching options for getting from Lisbon to Porto in Portugal.

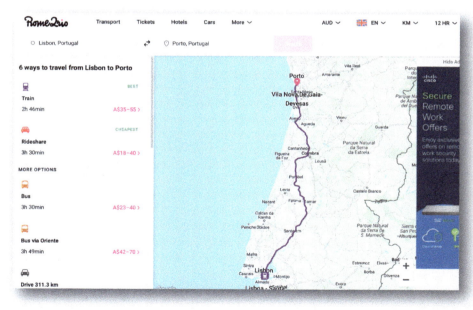

If I click on any of the options presented in the left sidebar, I then get a list of further options – for example, for the train option, I get a list of train times.

For transport that can be booked online in advance, there will be the option to jump to a booking site. Otherwise, the details of how to book with be shown.

16. Getting around

Travel by Car

If you need to grab a ride or rent a car, there are apps and online services that can help with that.

Uber is available in most major cities, for rides to wherever you need to get.

If you haven't used Uber before, make sure to set it up and try it out before you go – and, of course, make sure it is available at your travel destination/s.

Car rentals can be booked online and via an App.

We used a site affiliated with Booking.com – **rentalcars.com**, which also has an app.

Car rental can also be booked through other sites like Webjet, Expedia and other online travel agents.

Train Travel

If you are planning any train trips during your travels, there are some really handy apps for this.

Trainline and **Omio** are excellent apps for booking train tickets in Europe.

Omio also covers the US.

We have used **Trainline** to book tickets in Spain (and checked against Omio). It was easy to do. Note that we needed to provide passport details when booking.

16. Getting around

Organising Tours

There are lots of options for exploring and booking available tours at your travel destinations.

Two most commonly used apps/websites for exploring 'what to do' at your destinations and for booking tours are:

- **Viator** (at www.viator.com)

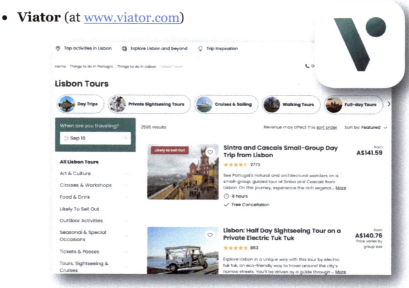

Tripadvisor (www.tripadvisor.com)

17. Accessories

Be Prepared

Don't forget the adaptors and cables!

Make sure you have all the different types of cables and adaptors that you need.

Consider a multi-port USB adaptor. I have one that offers the different international plugs that can be swapped in and out and provides 4 USB ports.

Another I have just purchased has all the different international plugs built into it and provides both USB-A and USB-C ports.

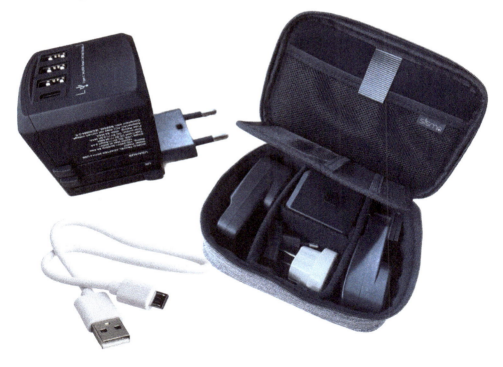

17. Accessories

Stay powered up (and safe) on the go!

Make sure you take at least one portable charger (or power bank) with you (along with a cable) – and make sure you keep it charged up after using it.

As mentioned in the in chapter 12. portable chargers offer a more secure way of charging your devices.

Plugging your device into public charging stations (via USB) can potentially be risky – especially if, when you plug in, you see a prompt on your device asking you to **Trust** another device - to which you should ALWAYS respond in the negative. If a power point is available, consider using this in preference to a USB port.

As mentioned earlier, my preference is to charge a portable charger at a public USB charging station, then use that charger to charge my device.

I carry a small purse with the charger and associated cables.

Below are a couple of pictures of a new portable charger that I purchased recently, one that has the charging cables build in to it. Very handy.

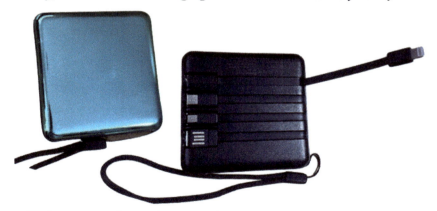

It will charge 2-3 phones between charges, has a capacity of 10,000 m/Ah, and a rating of 37Wh. And it shows a display of how much charge remains, which is very useful.

Always consider the Wh rating before carrying a portable/spare battery on a plane, as there are some restrictions that apply – although, in saying this, most portable charges will be well within limits.

17. Accessories

While there are International regulations about carrying portable batteries on planes, it is worth double-checking with your airline.

Here is what the Qantas website says about the international regulations on flying with batteries. Note that power banks must be in carry-on baggage.

What you can carry and requirements on how to pack

No more than 20 spare batteries in total, for personal use, are permitted per passenger. All other battery restrictions still apply e.g. no more than two spare lithium batteries exceeding 100Wh and up to 160Wh, are permitted and forms part of the total carried.

A combination of batteries may be carried e.g. 10 x 98Wh lithium ion + 2 x 138Wh lithium ion + 2 x 12V & 98Wh non-spillable + 6 x alkaline.

Note: Watt hours (Wh) are determined by multiplying the voltage (V) by the amp hours (Ah). ie. 12V x 5Ah = 60Wh

Important

All spare batteries and powerbanks must be as **carry-on** baggage only.

On Trains Trips

If you are going to be travelling by train, note that many trains have power points (and, maybe, USB ports).

So keep a power adaptor and cable in your bag if you are likely to need a charge while on a longer train trip.

AirPods / Headphones

For me, noise cancelling headphones are essential for any travel – especially on flights.

Not all headphones offer noise cancellation.

If yours don't offer this feature, consider purchasing a pair that do.

I also make sure to take my wired earphones – just in case something happens to my wireless pair.

17. Accessories

Accessory checklist

I'm sure there are a lot of other tech-related accessories that I have left out here. But for what it's worth, here's a bit of a checklist to get you started.

- ☐ Pin for popping out SIM Card
- ☐ A small case for carrying your SIM (if you need one)
- ☐ International power plugs
- ☐ Charging cables and adaptors
- ☐ Consider a multi-port charger
- ☐ Case for your accessories
- ☐ Portable chargers
- ☐ Camera adaptor (if you have a separate camera and want to import photos to an iPad or computer)
- ☐ Headphones – preferably noise cancelling
- ☐ Take a wired set or earphones for your phone - as a spare

18. Your Security While Travelling

Beware on Public Wi-Fi

Always be careful on any public Wi-Fi network that you use while travelling (or even in your home country) - especially airports, cafes, and other public places.

Even your Hotel or accommodation Wi-Fi could be risky.

What is the danger?

There are sometimes hackers, known as sniffers, who sit on public Wi-Fi networks and monitor the traffic, looking for data that is sent across the network in an unencrypted (i.e. unprotected) form. This data could include, as an example, login credentials for an email (or some other) account, or financial or identity information.

One way to ensure that your uploaded and downloaded data is encrypted as it travels across the network is to always ensure that the website you are using has a 'lock' on it – that the website's address (URL) starts with **https://**, not **http://**.

http:// sites are not secure, and you should never provide any sign-in credentials, financial, personal or identify information while on such a site.

$$\text{A}\text{A} \quad \text{🔒 commbank.com.au} \quad \circlearrowright$$

There is an even better way to make sure that your all internet data is secure while on such a Wi-Fi network.

Use a VPN

The best option for your security is to install something called a VPN – which stands for **Virtual Private Network.**

This VPN should be installed on all devices that will be connected to any public or potentially insecure Wi-Fi networks.

18. Your Security While Travelling

A VPN puts a protective 'layer' (or 'virtual tunnel') around your network connection – encrypting any data you upload or download, thereby creating a secure connection between your device/computer and the network to which it is attached. This prevents any hackers from accessing any of the data you sent or receive over that network.

A VPN also disguises your IP Address (which is your internet location), making your location invisible to others – and stopping any tracing of your device.

When you connect to a VPN, it will connect to the closest 'VPN Server' to your current location – to give the best speed for your internet data uploads and downloads.

Your VPN service provider will have VPN servers in various countries.

You can choose to manually select a 'VPN Server' from a particular country (instead of auto-connecting based on your current location) – including to a server from your home country. We'll talk about why you might do this shortly.

VPN apps are free to install and trial.

After the trial period, a monthly subscription will apply – and this will cover all the devices that use the VPN.

As with many Apps and services, you must set up an account with the VPN provider, make sure the provider's App is installed on each device, and then sign in to the same account on each device that is to use the VPN.

Then, when you need to use Wi-Fi on your travels, you make sure you have turned on this VPN.

Most VPN providers offer a month-by-month subscription, or a multi-month subscription (where the multi-month option is at a lower monthly cost).

18. Your Security While Travelling

Some suggestions on VPN

You can use Google to explore the best VPN options for the countries you will be visiting, by typing something like 'best VPN for travel in ....'.

For a long time, **ExpressVPN** has been a top-ranking option, offering services in countries not necessarily covered by other providers (e.g. China).

ExpressVPN will be my choice for our next trip later this year.

Another couple of VPNs that rank very well on all review sites are **NordVPN** and **VPN SurfShark**

I have also previously successfully used a popular option called **Private Internet Access (PIA)**, for a trip through Europe a few years ago.

Monthly subscriptions for VPN services range from $10-$25.

As mentioned earlier, the longer your subscription period, the cheaper the monthly rate.

A special advantage of a VPN

While you travel, you will probably find that your attempts to access your favourite streaming service from back home – e.g. Netflix, ABC iView – are unsuccessful.

This is due to 'geo-blocking' (also known as region blocking), where you are blocked from accessing content from a country that is different to your current location.

A very important benefit of using certain VPNs is that you will be able to 'pretend' you are connected in your home country, and therefore get around this geo-blocking to watch your favourite programs and content from home.

You do this by choosing to connect to a VPN Server located in your home country – and then trying to access your usual streaming content or geo-blocked website.

18. Your Security While Travelling

Not all VPNs are made equal for this – but ExpressVPN, NordVPN and VPN Surfshark are recommended options if this is something that you are likely to require.

Are your emails secure?

A particular example illustrates the danger of using a device on a public Wi-Fi network without VPN protection.

For some people, the way in which their email is retrieved by their Mail app could be giving away their email address and password to any 'sniffer' on the network.

If you are using an email account such as Bigpond, Optusnet, TPG, iiNet and many others, it is important to check if it is installed as a POP email account – and if it is, does the connection use something called SSL (which encrypts the connection with the mail server so that communications are protected).

For some people, their POP email account does not have this SSL switch turned on, which means their email address and password will travel over the Wi-Fi network without protection.

We won't attempt to cover where to find this setting for all the different mail providers and apps as part of this book.

If you do need assistance with this, contact your Telco for support – or make an appointment with iTandCoffee.

Always consider your Device Security

When you travel, it is especially important to consider your device security – both physical and virtual.

Make sure that, whenever you enter your device's passcode, you do this in a way that obscures the view for anyone else.

This includes considering any cameras that may be around you, as such cameras could record your passcode entry so that an unscrupulous person could use that recording.

18. Your Security While Travelling

If your device is stolen, it is essential to minimise the risk of the thief knowing or working out your passcode - as that passcode gives them a 'free ride' to wreak all sorts of havoc.

I see many clients who use 4 or 6 digit passcodes for their mobile phone, often of poor quality.

Some even choose the option of no passcode because they find the passcode an annoyance.

These are all very risky practices at the best of times.

With knowledge of your passcode, there are all sorts of things that a thief could access via your phone.

They will have access to the email accounts that are installed on that device – and can do all sorts of password resets, contact friends and family, and so much more.

They may even have access to your banking app. The mind boggles!

Choose a Strong Device Passcode / Password

One of the best protections for any device is a strong passcode or password. (Passcodes are usually just numbers, but a password includes letters and maybe symbols.)

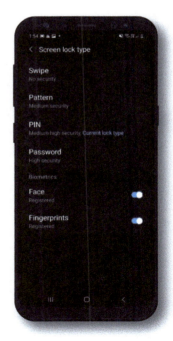

It is highly recommended that the passcode/password for your mobile device is as long as possible – and the recommendation is that it is at least 10 numeric or alpha-numeric characters. Mine is 12!

While you can also use any fingerprint or facial recognition capabilities offered by your device, you must still remember this passcode/password.

While having to enter a longer password may be an inconvenience at times for unlocking your device, it is well worth that inconvenience for the security it offers.

On my Samsung phone, the passcode/password for the device is set from **Settings -> Lock Screen -> Screen Lock Type.**

18. Your Security While Travelling

The most secure option is the Password option, including numbers and letters – at least 8. A long PIN (of many digits) also offers decent security.

I most definitely would not just use the **Swipe** option, as this offers no protection. A **Pattern** can offer medium security, but make sure it is not too simple.

Make sure your device locks when not in use

Make sure that authentication (i.e. Passcode/Password, fingerprint or face recognition) is required to unlock your device whenever the device's screen turns off – and that the screen turns off fairly quickly when the device is not in use.

This means that if someone picks up or steals your phone, it will hopefully already be locked. There are a couple of places where you set this up.

The delay before authentication is required after the display goes off is found (on my Samsung) in **Settings -> Lock Screen -> Secure lock settings**. Make sure this delay is as short as possible (e.g. max of 1 minute, less if you can tolerate it).

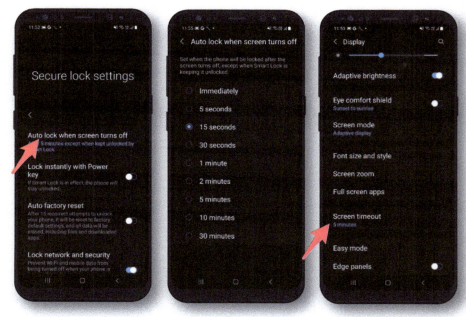

Also make sure that the display goes off fairly quickly when the device is not in use. This is controlled by the **Screen timeout** setting in **Settings ->**

18.   Your Security While Travelling

Display (see rightmost image above). Again, this should be as short a time as you can tolerate.

A shorter **Screen Timeout** setting will also save your battery, as the display is one of the biggest users of the battery.

As mentioned above, if you have set up facial recognition or a fingerprint, these can be used instead of the passcode/password most of the time.

But there will be times when you *must* enter the passcode/password – for example, when you change the password or Secure Lock settings.

Erase After Multiple Failed Unlock Attempts

Another protection to consider – especially when you travel - is a setting that will wipe your phone if someone tries over and over unlock your phone.

After 15 attempts, all your data will be erased, and the phone will be returned to factory settings.

On my Samsung, this setting is found in **Settings -> Lock Screen -> Secure lock settings**.

Turn on the **Auto factory reset** switch.

It is quite a drastic option to choose, but certainly offers a very effective protection in the case of theft.

Of course you would only choose such an option if your devices content is being regularly backed up or all your data is cloud based.

Prevent mobile data and Wi-Fi deactivation from lock screen

Another option worth turning on is the **Lock network and security** option that is shown on the screen above, in the **Secure lock settings** option.

If this setting is turned on, you will have a better chance of finding your device if it goes missing – allowing **Find My Mobile** to locate your device (and we'll cover this shortly).

18. Your Security While Travelling

Protecting your data and photos

For most of us, our photos are such an important part of our trips – and it is important to consider how to keep these photos safe and secure.

If your photos are only stored on your mobile device and something happens to that device, they could be lost forever.

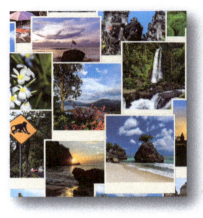

The best way to protect those precious photos and your data is to ensure that it is synced with a cloud service offered by Google or Microsoft (or perhaps Dropbox).

If you don't use any such service (or services) to sync your data (and even if you do), there is the option of using Google's Backup service.

We won't go into further detail about cloud services and how to use them – because that is a topic for another book.

But let's just touch on the backup option, which can be managed from **Settings -> Accounts and backup -> Back up data** (found under the **Google Drive** sub-heading, as indicated in the middle image below).

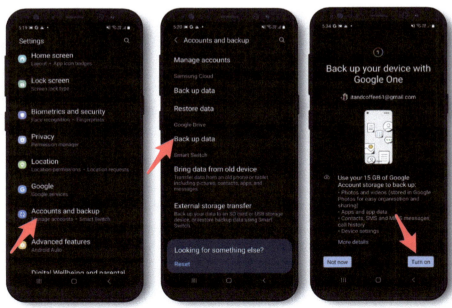

18.   Your Security While Travelling

As you can see in the rightmost image on the previous page, you get 15GB of storage for no cost, and then must pay a monthly fee if additional storage is needed for your device's data. Choose **Turn on** to activate the backup function.

Once you have chosen the **Turn on** option, you will see the option to **Back up now** to force the backup to occur right now.

Normally, your device will backup automatically if it has been idle and charging for 2 hours.

Scroll to the bottom of that screen to see the setting for controlling the backup's use of Mobile Data (as shown in the right screen above) – **Back up using mobile or metered Wi-Fi data**.

Turn this off when you are travelling – unless you have plenty of roaming mobile data that you are happy to use for backups.

Details of the data that is included in the backup is shown above that.

The backup process will only backup data that is not already syncing with your Google cloud.

These backup settings can also be managed from an app called **Google One**, which you can download from the Google Play store.

18.   Your Security While Travelling

Are your photos syncing?

An important consideration is whether your photos are being synced to any of your clouds – usually your Google Cloud or OneDrive (or perhaps Dropbox).

If they are not, then if something happens to your device, your photos could be lost.

Each cloud service provides a Setting that you can enable, to upload any photos taken by your device's camera to that cloud. In fact, you could upload or sync to multiple clouds!

For the purpose of this book, we will concentrate on Google's cloud and using the Backup settings in Google Photos / Settings to sync your photos.

You will see in the screen shot below left that my **Photos and videos** are already syncing using Google Photos

If my photos are not already syncing – or if I want to view the settings for this syncing – I tap on **Photos and videos** to get the middle screen below.

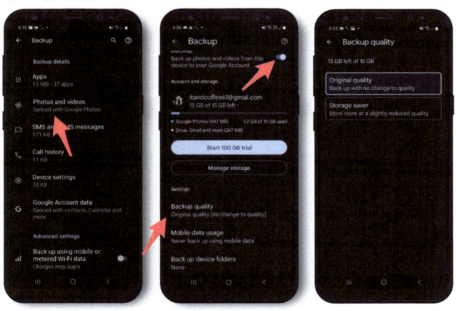

The switch at the top of that screen allows the backup/syncing of photos and videos in Google Photos to be enabled, and for the backup quality to be chosen.

Tap **Backup Quality** to view the options available (rightmost image above).

18. Your Security While Travelling

I have chosen to back up the **Original quality** versions (so I don't lose any quality if something happens to my phone)– but may run out of space if I take a lot of photos.

I would then need to purchase more storage if I want to keep full resolution versions. Or I would have to choose **Storage Saver** to free up space (and risk losing my full resolution photos if my device is lost/broken).

Another option to look at in this area is the **Mobile data usage** option.

Even if you have chosen to turn off Mobile Data use by the backup, there may still be mobile data used for syncing your photos.

In the **Mobile data usage** option, it is best to select **No data** while you travel – or at least choose one of the other limits for your photo uploads.

Ensuring you can find a lost device

If you are unlucky enough to lose your Android device while travelling, there is feature which – if enabled – can allow you to potentially track your device, play a sound to try to find it, lock it with a message on the screen (e.g. providing a number that the finder can call), and erase it remotely.

It is the **Find My Device** feature associated with your Google account and device.

Go to **Settings -> Google -> Find my Device** and turn On the switch at the top.

18. Your Security While Travelling

By turning on this feature you may be able to locate the device even if it was muted before you misplaced it, playing a sound that hopefully allows you to find it.

Finding a lost device

Locating a lost device can be done from the **Find My Device** app on another person's Android device, or by visiting the website **myaccount.google.com/find-your-phone**.

In in both cases, you will need to sign in to your Google account – so will need to know your email address and password.

Below shows the screen that I get when I look for my Samsung phone using the website, showing my device on a map and offering the options (in left sidebar) to **PLAY SOUND, SECURE DEVICE**, or **ERASE DEVICE.**

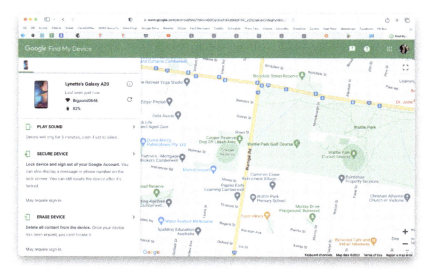

If you think your device is somewhere nearby, try the **Play Sound** option – which will loudly play a ring tone for 5 minutes even if your device is muted.

If your device is not nearby – or looks to be stolen, choose the **Secure Device** option.

This option allows you to provide a message that is displayed on the screen for whoever has the device. You could provide a contact phone number, on the off chance that a good Samaritan has your device.

And if you really think your device is stolen – and perhaps at risk of being accessed by the thief – then choose the **Erase Device** option.

19. Must-have apps

So many apps!

Of course, there are so many apps to choose from when it comes to travel.

We have already mentioned many in earlier chapters and will mention a few more shortly.

Here is a summarised list of some of the more popular apps.

- ☐ Tripit – travel planner / itinerary.
- ☐ Trainline, Omio – train tickets.
- ☐ Rome2Rio – options for getting from A to B (plus bookings).
- ☐ Booking.com – accommodation, flights, car rentals.
- ☐ AirBNB – accommodation.
- ☐ Expedia.com - accommodation, flights, car rentals.
- ☐ Skyscanner – aggregator of flight, hotel, car rental options.
- ☐ Tripadviser – all things travel – hotels, restaurants, tours.
- ☐ Trivago – aggregator of hotel options.
- ☐ Viator – what to see and do.
- ☐ Citymapper – Public transport app and maps.
- ☐ Visit a City – what to do.
- ☐ Google Translate - offline or online translations.
- ☐ Microsoft Translator – online translations only.
- ☐ Airline app/s.
- ☐ Google Maps – maps and navigation.
- ☐ Airalo – data only eSIMs.
- ☐ Mobile banking app/s.
- ☐ Insurance Company app (if applicable).
- ☐ Sygic – maps and navigation.
- ☐ Maps.ME – maps and navigation.
- ☐ Uber – car rides.
- ☐ XE Currency – currency conversion.
- ☐ Camera+ - fantastic photo optimization.
- ☐ Adobe Scan – scanning using your mobile.

19. Must-have apps

- ☐ Adobe Fill & Sign – fill forms and sign forms/documents.
- ☐ A good Weather app (e.g. Yahoo Weather).
- ☐ Flush - public toilet finder!!

Scanning documents

Make sure you have a scanning app on your phone, for any situation where you need to scan a physical page (or pages) to send to someone.

An excellent free option is Adobe Scan. Another is Microsoft's Lens app.

These apps are not just relevant to travel. They are must-haves for any mobile device and can save you from ever having to fire up that printer/scanner ever again.

Signing documents while away

An app mentioned above is a 'must-have' for travelling – in fact, for any time.

I use it whenever I need to fill in and sign a form.

It is the **Adobe Fill and Sign** app, which allows you to so easily fill and sign forms and documents without needing to involve a printer or scanner.

You can even save you signature for re-use whenever it is needed.

20. What about money

There are a few key things to think about in relation to money and technology when you are travelling – as well as some key things that are not really technology related, but that are worthy of a mention.

Do you get SMS Authorisations?

As mentioned earlier, if you get SMS authorisations from your bank, make sure you have access to your home SIM for texted codes. As also covered earlier, you will also need to have access to International Roaming to receive any such SMS.

Let the bank know your plans

Make sure you notify your bank that you will be away.

Otherwise, your use of your credit/debit card while overseas could result in your account being frozen due to suspected fraud.

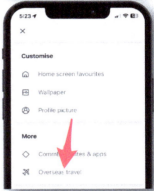

For some banks such a notification can be done from within the bank's mobile App.

Such options may be found under the **Cards** option of the banking app, or (as for Commbank) in the **Settings** area.

Screens from the Commbank app are shown on the right.

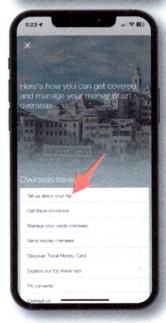

Travel money

If you use your usual credit or debit card while travelling, you will find that every transaction incurs an international transaction fee – and the cost of these fees can mount up over time.

Another option to consider is a special travel debit card, one that you load up with the currency (or

20.   What about money

currencies) you will need while you travel. This card can then be topped up as needed.

Several banks offer such travel money cards. Westpac's gets the best review for fees/etc. Here's a choice.com article on the topic: www.choice.com.au/travel/money/travel-money/articles/travel-money-cards

I use the **Commbank Travel Card** because I am a Commbank customer – and I can manage this card from within my usual Commbank app.

It is so quick & easy to transfer money immediately, between my normal account and the travel card – and choose a currency when I do this. The exchange rate that applies at the time shows.

I add money to this travel card account on a regular basis before the trip, on days when the exchange rate is good.

I also have a **Qantas Travel Money** card – a debit card that is linked to my Qantas Frequent Flyer account. This will also have a bit of money on it as backup.

For the Qantas card, there is an app that allows easy top-up of funds of any currency. The downside of the Qantas card is that there is a 1 day delay for free top-ups (using the bank transfer option).

Wise is another highly rated travel money card to consider.

Just make sure before you go that you have any relevant app associated with your Travel Money Card, and that you know how to top up.

Just as a note, Commbank provided me with two Travel cards, so that I have a spare – just in case!

Tracking the exchange rate

If you are looking to load up a travel money card in advance of your trip – on days when the exchange rate is good – it is worth setting up currency exchange rate alerts.

I get an alert each morning that advises of the day's exchange rate. That alert pops up as a notification and can also arrive in an email.

20. What about money

The app I have used to get my daily alert is the **Wise** app – the app associated with the Wise travel money card. You don't have use one of their cards to take advantage of this feature.

Here are another couple of apps that provide alerts:

- **CurrencyXT**– no need to create an account to get rate alerts.
- **XE Currency** – you must create account to get rate alerts.

All of the above-mentioned apps allow you to view how the exchange rate tracks over time.

Note. **XE Currency** has been my 'go to' app for currency conversion for over 12 years.

You still need a credit card for certain things

It is important to note that, while your travel money debit card will be accepted in most places, there are a few circumstances where you might need a credit card instead.

For example, when checking in for a hotel room, or when hiring a car, you may have to provide a credit card for incidentals.

So, make sure you take your usual credit card as well – or perhaps take an alternative credit card to your usual card, one that has a limited credit limit.

Travel Insurance

Does your credit card provide travel insurance with it?

Some credit cards offer such insurance, so make sure you investigate this option. It could save you lots.

21. Your Travel Snaps

Capturing those holiday memories

What will you use to take photos while you travel? Most of us tend you just take our mobile phones as our camera.

We have already talked about a couple of things relating to your photos – storage and backups or syncing.

But let's look at some other things to consider.

Make sure Camera saves locations

One of the best reasons for using your smartphone to take photos is that such photos can record the exact location of the photo.

This is so useful when you travel because it allows for viewing of your travel snaps on a map and later allows you to work out where they were taken.

Go to **Settings -> Location -> App permissions -> Camera**.

Make sure that the option **ALLOW only while using app** is selected.

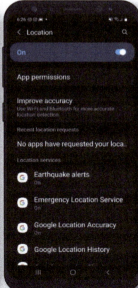

21. Your Travel Snaps

Use Camera for signs, timetables

Remember to use your phone's camera to capture timetables and signs, so that you can refer back to them as needed.

Organising photos as you go

If you have time at the end of each day, or when in transit, it is well worth going through recent photos and cleaning up any that you don't need, or applying edits where needed.

Create an album or albums of your best ones.

And if you plan to make a photo book when you return, choose the best photos that you will use in that book and add them to an album for that purpose.

If you use a service like Snapfish for making photo books, you can even progressively upload your chosen photos (when you have Wi-Fi) – so that you don't need to go through this process when you return.

22. Entertainment

Movies and TV Series on your device

If you have sufficient storage on your phone or tablet, it may be worth downloading some movies, TV series or documentaries – so that you can watch them without requiring internet.

Some streaming services allow you to download content. Or there is always the option to purchase content from the **Google TV** app.

For your listening pleasure

If you have Spotify, make sure your favourite music is downloaded so that you don't need internet to listen to it. You will need a paid account to do this.

Again, you will also need sufficient storage for this downloaded music.

Another great option for travelling is **Podcasts** – which are usually completely free. This can be via Spotify, Google Podcasts, or other podcast apps.

Again, make sure you download a set of podcasts before you go, or when you have access to Wi-Fi.

Reading

If you are an avid reader, carrying a range of books with you as you travel can really add to the weight and bulk of your luggage.

An alternative option that allows you to take as many books as you like – without impacting your luggage – is to read **eBooks**.

22. Entertainment

eBooks can be read on your Android device, using an eReader like the Kindle app.

I recently purchased a **Kindle** device for my eBooks. It is very light, has a battery that lasts for about 10 weeks, can be read in the sun and on the beach, and is even waterproof.

I will download a set of books in advance and as we travel (when on Wi-Fi).

There are a couple other key benefits of eBooks.

You can download samples of books to read the first set of pages, to see if you like it before purchasing. And many of the classics are free to download and read.

Other Entertainment

Finally, think about downloading some timewasters from the Play Store – games and puzzles that help to fill in time in transit, and while waiting.

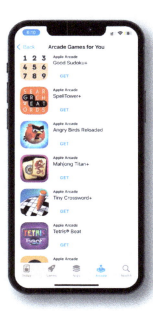

Some good examples are:

- Solitaire
- Sudoku
- Wordle
- Quordle
- Jigsaws
- Crosswords
- Threes
- Tetris
- Angry Birds

Appendix A
International Roaming with Telstra

Telstra offers two main services for International Roaming, for most people with monthly post-paid Telstra plans – **International Day Pass** and **Pay As You Go.**

International Day Pass

https://www.telstra.com.au/content/dam/tcom/help/critical-information-summaries/personal/mobile/international-roaming/International-Day-Pass.pdf

- Pay per day - $5 (New Zealand) or $10 for long list of other countries (check the countries that it covers before you leave).
- You are only charged on days where you use your phone, send a text, or use mobile data.
- On days you use the day pass, you have unlimited calls/texts & 1GB data
- Data is automatically topped up if you use > 1gb in a day, and top-up is then valid for 31 days. The 1GB daily allowance does not roll over – it expires each day.
- Activate (or de-activate) Day Pass using My Telstra App.
- You will receive data usage warnings via text, at 50%, 85%, 100%.
- The 'day' is based on AEST, not local OS time - AEST 0:00 TO 24:00.

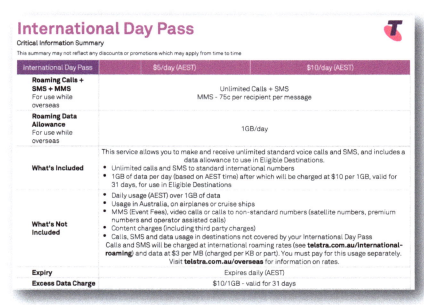

International Day Pass

Critical Information Summary

This summary may not reflect any discounts or promotions which may apply from time to time

International Day Pass	$5/day (AEST)	$10/day (AEST)
Roaming Calls + SMS + MMS For use while overseas	Unlimited Calls + SMS MMS - 75c per recipient per message	
Roaming Data Allowance For use while overseas	1GB/day	
What's Included	This service allows you to make and receive unlimited standard voice calls and SMS, and includes a data allowance to use in Eligible Destinations. • Unlimited calls and SMS to standard international numbers • 1GB of data per day (based on AEST time) after which will be charged at $10 per 1GB, valid for 31 days, for use in Eligible Destinations	
What's Not Included	• Daily usage (AEST) over 1GB of data • Usage in Australia, on airplanes or cruise ships • MMS (Event Fees), video calls or calls to non-standard numbers (satellite numbers, premium numbers and operator assisted calls) • Content charges (including third party charges) • Calls, SMS and data usage in destinations not covered by your International Day Pass Calls and SMS will be charged at international roaming rates (see **telstra.com.au/international-roaming**) and data at $3 per MB (charged per KB or part). You must pay for this usage separately. Visit **telstra.com.au/overseas** for information on rates.	
Expiry	Expires daily (AEST)	
Excess Data Charge	$10/1GB - valid for 31 days	

Appendix A
International Roaming with Telstra

Countries covered by the $10 Day Pass are:

Argentina, Austria, Bangladesh, Belarus, Belgium, Brazil, Brunei, Bulgaria, Cambodia, Canada, Chile, China, Colombia, Croatia, Cyprus, Czech Republic, Denmark, Ecuador, Egypt, Estonia, Fiji, Finland, France, Germany, Greece, Hong Kong, Hungary, India, Indonesia, Ireland, Israel, Italy, Japan, Laos, Latvia, Lithuania, Luxembourg, Macau, Macedonia, Malaysia, Mexico, Nauru, Netherlands, Norway, Papua New Guinea, Philippines, Poland, Portugal, Qatar, Romania, Russia, Saudi Arabia, Serbia, Singapore, Slovak Rep., Slovenia, Solomon Islands, South Africa, South Korea, Spain, Sri Lanka, Sweden, Switzerland, Taiwan, Thailand, Turkey, Ukraine, UAE, UK, USA, Uruguay, Vanuatu, Vietnam

IMPORTANT NOTE: Cruise ships are excluded from Day Pass - PAYG rates apply.

Pay As You Go (PAYG)

Be very careful of using PAYG. You need to make sure you know how to avoid unexpected calls and data costs.

Never use PAYG if mobile data and data roaming are active.

- You pay per mb of data ($3/MB) and for each call ($2-$3.50 per min) & sent SMS (75¢ per standard text, >$3/mb for MMS).
- This can result in huge expense, so beware.
- Rates for calls vary depending on location.
- I suggest only using this if you want to do occasional SMS's (or if you have no other option).
- Rates vary based on overseas location – here is where to check your destination's costs:
  https://www.telstra.com.au/international-roaming/lightbox-international-roaming-rates-map

Appendix A
International Roaming with Telstra

Here are some examples of the costs for the different countries, as applied at the time of writing this book. As you can see, Data (which includes messages that use MMS) is very expensive. And the cost of any incoming or outgoing phone call can end up being well above the Day Pass cost (if that is an option for you).

ENGLAND Add to itinerary	
› Check network availability	
Make and receive a call	$2.00 per minute
Send SMS	75c
Receive SMS	Free
Data	$3.00 per MB charged per KB
Send MMS	Standard charges* + $3.00 per MB
Receive MMS	$3.00 per MB
MessageBank®	$2.00 per minute

SPAIN Add to itinerary	
› Check network availability	
Make and receive a call	$3.50 per minute
Send SMS	75c
Receive SMS	Free
Data	$3.00 per MB charged per KB
Send MMS	Standard charges* + $3.00 per MB
Receive MMS	$3.00 per MB
MessageBank®	$3.50 per minute

PORTUGAL Add to itinerary	
› Check network availability	
Make and receive a call	$2.00 per minute
Send SMS	75c
Receive SMS	Free
Data	$3.00 per MB charged per KB
Send MMS	Standard charges* + $3.00 per MB
Receive MMS	$3.00 per MB
MessageBank®	$2.00 per minute

Managing International Roaming with Telstra App

- Get the **My Telstra** app from the Play Store. (Note. We show the iPhone version of the app below, but the Android version is the same.)
- Activate/manage roaming via this **My Telstra** app.
- Select **Services** at bottom, then the mobile service, then **Extras**

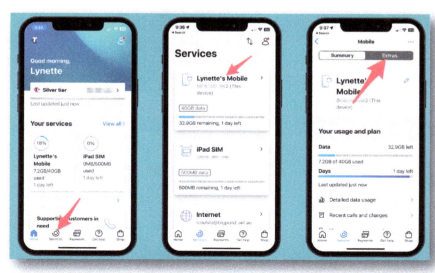

Appendix A
International Roaming with Telstra

- Choose the **International Roaming** option to see what settings are available.
- You will hopefully see the **International Roaming** switch and a separate **International Day Pass** switch.

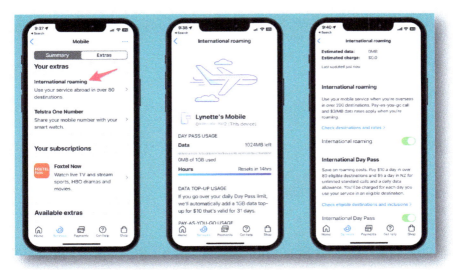

- If **International Day Pass** is turned off and **International** Roaming is on, **PAYG** applies if there are any calls, outgoing texts or mobile data used.

Pre-paid Roaming Packs (for pre-paid SIM)

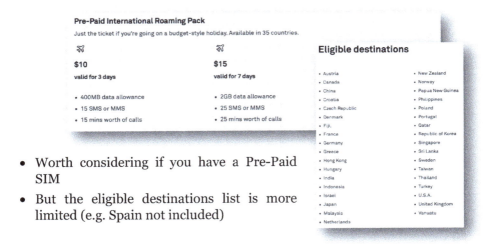

- Worth considering if you have a Pre-Paid SIM
- But the eligible destinations list is more limited (e.g. Spain not included)

Appendix B
International Roaming with Optus

Optus $5 Roaming Add-On

https://www.optus.com.au/mobile/plans/international-roaming

- Optus has similar offerings to Telstra.
- But Optus is half the price and has a more generous data allowance (5GB per day).
- The **Roaming Add-on** is enabled via the **My Optus** app.
- It offers unlimited standard talk & text and 5GB of data per day, for 100+ countries.

The key difference in the Optus offering is that

- $5 Roaming Add-on must be enabled on each day that you want to use it – from the app.
- Or you can choose a 7-day option for $35, so that you don't have to enable each day.
- Wi-Fi connection is not needed to enable the add-on for the day – so you can do this on the go.
- Availability depends on your plan. Available to Optus Choice Plus, Optus Plus Family & Optus Plus

Set up your $5 Roaming Add-on

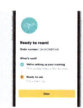

Open My Optus App to check your roaming options under:

Service > Add-ons > International Roaming

Your roaming add-on starts on activation it so it's best to buy it on arrival, at your destination.
(No Wi-Fi required).

Choose and buy a roaming add-on. Grab your bags – you're good to go.

As you return home to Australia, roaming will automatically switch off. Thanks for roaming with us.

Appendix B
International Roaming with Optus

- Check if your destination is covered:

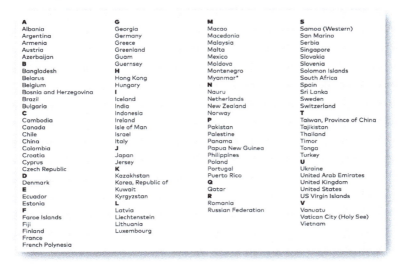

A	G	M	S
Albania	Georgia	Macao	Samoa (Western)
Argentina	Germany	Macedonia	San Marino
Armenia	Greece	Malaysia	Serbia
Austria	Greenland	Malta	Singapore
Azerbaijan	Guam	Mexico	Slovakia
B	Guernsey	Moldova	Slovenia
Bangladesh	**H**	Montenegro	Solomon Islands
Belarus	Hong Kong	Myanmar*	South Africa
Belgium	Hungary	**N**	Spain
Bosnia and Herzegovina	**I**	Nauru	Sri Lanka
Brazil	Iceland	Netherlands	Sweden
Bulgaria	India	New Zealand	Switzerland
C	Indonesia	Norway	**T**
Cambodia	Ireland	**P**	Taiwan, Province of China
Canada	Isle of Man	Pakistan	Tajikistan
Chile	Israel	Palestine	Thailand
China	Italy	Panama	Timor
Colombia	**J**	Papua New Guinea	Tonga
Croatia	Japan	Philippines	Turkey
Cyprus	Jersey	Poland	**U**
Czech Republic	**K**	Portugal	Ukraine
D	Kazakhstan	Puerto Rico	United Arab Emirates
Denmark	Korea, Republic of	**Q**	United Kingdom
E	Kuwait	Qatar	United States
Ecuador	Kyrgyzstan	**R**	US Virgin Islands
Estonia	**L**	Romania	**V**
F	Latvia	Russian Federation	Vanuatu
Faroe Islands	Liechtenstein		Vatican City (Holy See)
Fiji	Lithuania		Vietnam
Finland	Luxembourg		
France			
French Polynesia			

- Different costs apply for some plans (non Choice Plus) plans.
- Make sure you know what plan you are on and consider an upgrade if you don't qualify.

Roaming Options on non Choice Plus Plans

You have two options for roaming with either the $10 Optus Roaming Pass or standard roaming rates.

$10 Optus Roaming Pass

Get 1GB data and unlimited national talk and text for 24 hours to over 100 Zone 1 destinations.

Open My Optus App to check your roaming options under:
Service > Settings > International Roaming

The $10 Roaming pass is available to customers on selected postpaid mobile plans (excluding Choice Plus plans which are eligible for $5 roaming). On plans with roaming inclusions you'll roll-over to a $10 Optus Roaming Pass if you continue roaming in eligible destinations, once you've finished your plan's inclusions.

Standard Roaming Rates

Roam and get charged standard roaming rates. Pay per minute for calls, sending SMS, MMS sent & received, $1/MB for data in Zone 1 & 2, and $2/MB data use in Aerospace & Maritime.

Open My Optus App to check your roaming options under:
Service > Settings > International Roaming

Available to customers on selected postpaid mobile plans (excluding Choice Plus plans which are eligible for $5 roaming). Explore all **roaming rates**.

- For other plans, cost is $10 per day for the **Roaming Pass** (instead of $5)
- Check your roaming options from the **Service** option of the app (along bottom of app), **Service > Settings > International Roaming**
- Note that PAYG rates apply if the Roaming Add-on is not available.

Appendix B
International Roaming with Optus

Pay as You Go

- If you are not using the daily add-on/pass, PAYG Rates apply - $1-$2 per MB for data, $1.5-$4 /min for talk, 50¢-$1 per sent SMS.

Postpaid roaming rates

Location	Data	Talk	Text
Zone 1	$1/MB	$1.50/min	50c/SMS
Zone 2	$1/MB	$1.50/min	50c/SMS
Zone 3	$2/MB	$4.00/min	$1/SMS

- Determine the Zone/costs applicable to your travel destination at *https://www.optus.com.au/mobile/plans/international-roaming/postpaid-rates*

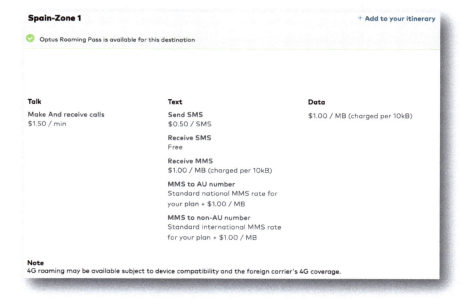

Spain-Zone 1   + Add to your itinerary

✅ Optus Roaming Pass is available for this destination

Talk

Make And receive calls
$1.50 / min

Text

Send SMS
$0.50 / SMS

Receive SMS
Free

Receive MMS
$1.00 / MB (charged per 10kB)

MMS to AU number
Standard national MMS rate for
your plan + $1.00 / MB

MMS to non-AU number
Standard international MMS rate
for your plan + $1.00 / MB

Data

$1.00 / MB (charged per 10kB)

Note
4G roaming may be available subject to device compatibility and the foreign carrier's 4G coverage.

Appendix B
International Roaming with Optus

Prepaid Roaming Options

https://www.optus.com.au/mobile/plans/international-roaming/prepaid

- If you have pre-paid SIM, you also have $5 and $35 roaming options, but there are different inclusions to those for post-paid accounts.

- $5 roaming has 1GB of data, 100 texts and up to 100 mins talk per day.
- $35 roaming has 7GB of data, 700 texts and up to 700 minutes per 7 days.
- Only available for Zone 1 countries
- Credits are also available - $10 talk credit, $20 data-only credit for limited destinations. See link above for further details.

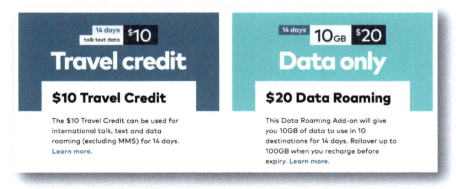

Handy article about Optus Roaming

- www.whistleout.com.au/MobilePhones/Guides/Optus-international-roaming-everything-you-need-to-know

Appendix C
International Roaming with Vodafone

$5 Roaming

https://www.vodafone.com.au/plans/international-roaming

- Like Optus, Vodafone offers a $5/day option.
- The key difference with Vodafone is that it that uses your usual plan's call and data inclusions.
- Use the **My Vodafone app** to check and manage this.

How $5 Roaming works

$5 extra a day
You'll only be charged $5 extra a day in addition to your plan fees when you use your included data, make or receive a call or send an SMS.

Use your plan overseas
Use your plan's included data, calls and texts in over 100 countries. Excludes data capped at speeds of up to 1.5Mbps, 2Mbps, 10Mbps and 25Mbps. If you go over your included data limit, we'll automatically add 1GB for $5.

Easy activation
$5 Roaming should be activated already for you. Just switch on your phone in an eligible country. You can check and manage roaming through My Vodafone.

- Check if $5 Roaming is offered for your destination.

■ $5 Roaming ■ Pay As You Go Roaming

Appendix C
International Roaming with Vodafone

Pay As You Go

https://www.vodafone.com.au/support/plans/roaming-rates

- PAYG option is also available - $1/min, 75¢ for outbound SMS, $1 per MB data.
- See above map for countries that only offer this option.
- As for other Telco's, be very cautious of turning on Mobile Data and Roaming if you choose the PAYG option.

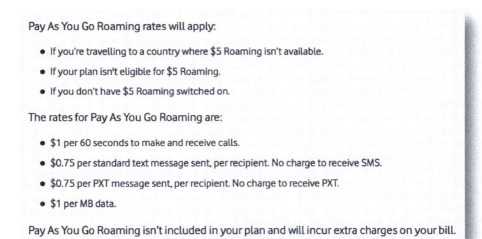

Pay As You Go Roaming rates will apply:

- If you're travelling to a country where $5 Roaming isn't available.
- If your plan isn't eligible for $5 Roaming.
- If you don't have $5 Roaming switched on.

The rates for Pay As You Go Roaming are:

- $1 per 60 seconds to make and receive calls.
- $0.75 per standard text message sent, per recipient. No charge to receive SMS.
- $0.75 per PXT message sent, per recipient. No charge to receive PXT.
- $1 per MB data.

Pay As You Go Roaming isn't included in your plan and will incur extra charges on your bill.

Prepaid Roaming

https://www.vodafone.com.au/prepaid/plans/international-roaming

- If you have (or get) a Pre-paid SIM from Vodafone, you can choose a Prepaid Roaming Add-on

Appendix C
International Roaming with Vodafone

- Pre-pay for calls and data – e.g. $5 for 1 day, with 25 mins talk, 30 outbound texts and 200MB data; $35 for 7 days, 200 mins talk, 300 texts, 2GB data.
- Recharge using a text code.
- Make sure to check if your destination is covered.

There are over 80 countries where you can use a Prepaid Roaming Add-on. See the full list of countries below. These countries may change from time to time, so it's important to check that your chosen country is included.

Prepaid Roaming Add-on countries

Cruising

- Vodafone may have Maritime Roaming rates for your cruise ship.
- $5 per mins talk, 75¢ per outbound texts, $1 per MB data.

Maritime Roaming

Maritime Roaming rates may apply if you're on a cruise, even if it's only around Australia. On selected cruise ships, you can make calls, send text messages and use data at the following rates:

- $5 per 60 seconds to make and receive calls.
- $0.75 per standard text message sent, per recipient. No charge to receive SMS.
- $1.00 per MB.

We have roaming partnerships with Telenor Maritime and Wireless Maritime Services. Check their websites to see if Maritime Roaming is available on your cruise ship. If it's available, on-board Wi-Fi is an alternative to using mobile data.

www.ingramcontent.com/pod-product-compliance
Lightning Source LLC
LaVergne TN
LVHW011802070326
832902LV00025B/4607